Buckle Down™

Reading

Level 6

2nd Edition

This book belongs to: _____

Buckle Down
Publishing

A Haights Cross Communications ® Company

Helping your schoolhouse meet the standards of the statehouse™

Acknowledgments

Photograph of Melissa Poe carrying an Olympic torch, from the Kids F.A.C.E. website, reprinted by permission of Trish Poe.

"Big Feet" by Rick Zollo, adapted from the Cherokee folktale.

Excerpt from "Rip Van Winkle" from *The Sketch Book* by Washington Irving, adapted by Torie Dial.

Excerpt from *Number the Stars* by Lois Lowry. Copyright © 1989 by Lois Lowry. Reprinted by permission of Houghton Mifflin Company. All rights reserved.

Excerpt from "Goblin Market" from *Goblin Market and Other Poems* by Christina G. Rossetti. Public domain.

Excerpt adapted from *Hamlet* by William Shakespeare. Public domain.

Excerpt from *Up From Slavery* by Booker T. Washington. Public domain.

Excerpt from "The Red Girl" from *Annie John* by Jamaica Kincaid. Copyright © 1985 by Jamaica Kincaid. Reprinted by permission of Farrar, Straus and Giroux, LLC.

"Fast Food Chain" by John Hansen. Copyright ©1995 by John Hansen. Reprinted by permission of the author.

"Lengths of Time" by Phyllis McGinley, copyright © 1965, 1966 by Phyllis McGinley. Copyright renewed © 1993, 1994 by Patricia Blake. First appeared in *Wonderful Time*, published by J. B. Lippincott (now HarperCollins Publishers). Reprinted by permission of Curtis Brown, Ltd.

Illustration from *Goblin Market and Other Poems* by Christina Rosetti, is reprinted courtesy of the University of Oxford and Google Print Programme. Public domain.

Drawing of a sarcophagus at the Louvre Museum reprinted courtesy of Wikipedia, http://en.wikipedia.org.

Photograph of Forgotten Home © Shaun Lowe/iStockphoto.

Photograph of Ace of Hearts © Suprijono Suharjoto/iStockphoto.

Photograph of Training Wheels © tiburonstudios/iStockphoto.

Photograph of Teddy Bear with Yellow Flower © Stratesigns/iStockphoto.

Illustration of sea serpent © jsnover/Stockxpert.

Photograph of Young Hands at Piano 1 © Robert Rushton/iStockphoto.

Photograph of four leaf clover © Yang Yin/iStockphoto.

Photograph of horseshoe © Michaela Fehiker/iStockphoto.

Photograph of I See Ghosts © Duncan Walker/iStockphoto.

Illustration of Hamlet in the Presence of His Father's Ghost, by John Gilbert, reprinted courtesy of Wikimedia, http://commons.wikipedia.org.

Photograph of Samuel Clemens (Mark Twain) is reprinted courtesy of Wikimedia, http://commons.wikipedia.org.

Excerpt from "Player Piano," from *The Carpentered Hen and Other Tame Creatures* by John Updike, copyright © 1982 by John Updike. Used by permission of Alfred A. Knopf, a division of Random House, Inc.

Photograph of General Lewis A. Armistead reprinted courtesy of the Gettysburg National Military Park.

Portrait of Maj. Gen. Winfield S. Hancock reprinted courtesy of the Library of Congress, Prints and Photographs Division, LC-B8172-1877.

Daguerrotype of Washington Irving, ca. 1855, by John Plumbe is reprinted courtesy of the Library of Congress, Prints and Photographs Division, LC-USZ62-110044 DLC.

Photograph of John Muir, circa 1902, reprinted courtesy of the Library of Congress American Memory website, LC-USZ62-52000.

Portrait of Ueshiba Morihei, founder of Aikido, artist and year of origin unknown. Public domain.

Photograph of Lois Lowry by Amanda Smith.

Photograph of Abell 2218, a cluster of galaxies, as photographed by the Hubble Space Telescope is reprinted courtesy of NASA.

Excerpt adapted from "The Great Sea-Serpent" by Hans Christian Anderson, from *Scribner's Monthly*, Vol. 3, Issue 3. Public domain.

"The Poet Pencil" by Jesus Carlos Soto Morfin, translated by Judith Infante, copyright © Judith Infante. Used by permission.

"An Encounter with an Interviewer" by Mark Twain, adapted for the stage by Mike Acton.

Every effort has been made by the publisher to locate each owner of the copyrighted material reprinted in this publication and to secure the necessary permissions. If there are any questions regarding the use of these materials, the publisher will take appropriate corrective measures to acknowledge ownership in future publications.

ISBN-10: 0-7836-4997-5
ISBN-13: 978-0-7836-4997-9

2BDUS06RD01   3 4 5 6 7 8 9 10

Senior Editor: Brendan Wolfe; Project Editor: Amy Walsh; Editor: Steven Ramirez; Production Editor: Jennifer Rapp; Cover Design: Christina Nantz; Cover Graphic Designer: Christina Kroemer; Production Director: Jennifer Booth; Art Director: Chris Wolf; Graphic Designer: Mark Nodland; Composition: Wyndham Books.

TABLE OF CONTENTS

To the Teacher:

Standards and Skills are listed for each lesson in the table of contents and for each page in the shaded gray bars that run across the tops of the pages in the workbook (see the example at right). These codes identify the Buckle Down Learning Standards and Skills covered on a given page.

Introduction

You read for many reasons. Of course, you read textbooks and other materials for school. Perhaps you also enjoy books, magazines, or Internet sites about things that really interest you, such as your favorite musicians or college basketball teams. Sometimes you read to find information, such as how to play a new video game. Or maybe you enjoy curling up with a good mystery or adventure story—just for fun.

From time to time, you will be asked to use your reading skills for a special purpose, such as taking a reading test. In some ways, the work you do on these tests will be similar to the other reading assignments you do in school. In other ways, it might be very, very different.

This Book Can Help

This book has been written to help you review and practice important reading skills. These skills will help you better understand the things you read—whether you are reading for school or for fun.

You'll also practice using these skills on the types of reading passages and questions often found on reading tests. You'll learn important test-taking tips, too. These tips will give you a better understanding of the test-taking process and will help you do your best on test day.

Reading or Liver?

Some people love to read. Others would rather eat cold liver and onions than open a book. Most people who dislike reading usually feel this way because they don't think they are very good at it. Sometimes reading can seem more like work than fun.

If you haven't had much success with reading in the past, it's almost certainly *not* because you can't do well at it. You probably just need some practice. And who knows? Once you are reading more and improving your skills, you might just discover that you really enjoy reading after all.

The Secret

How did Michelle Wie become a great golfer? How did Beyoncé Knowles become a Grammy-winning singer? How did Tony Hawk become the world's best skateboarder? The answer to all of these questions is the same: practice, practice, practice.

Reading is just like any other skill: You can only get better with practice. No matter how good a reader you are, practice can help you become even better.

You might not always enjoy your assignments in school, but when you get a note from a friend, you can hardly wait to rip it open and start reading. The point is, reading can be easy if you want to do it.

Perhaps you enjoy reading comic strips. Or maybe you like fashion articles or science-fiction books. Are you into playing soccer, listening to music, drawing, stargazing, or just hanging out with your friends? Whatever your "thing" is, someone has probably written about it. So, find material you will enjoy reading—and dig in.

Test-Taking Tips

You can think of a reading test as a game. Like any other game, getting a good score depends on your natural ability, but it also depends on three other important things:

- how much you have practiced.
- how good your strategy is.
- how well you stay cool, calm, and focused.

Here are some general tips to think about as you practice playing the Reading Test Game.

 ## TIP 1: Do a "first read" of the passage.

The first time you read a passage, read every word. Don't skip over anything. By reading every word, you'll gain a clear understanding of the "big picture," or what the passage is *mostly* about. You don't have to remember every detail. Just get a feel for the major ideas, how they are ordered in the passage, and the locations of important details.

It's okay to slow down and go back over a difficult idea, but don't get stuck. Keep moving until you come to the end of the passage.

 ## TIP 2: Learn how to answer different kinds of questions.

Test questions come in many different styles. This book contains the types of questions and passages that are most often seen on reading tests. Each lesson will show you how to answer a certain question type and will give you plenty of opportunities to practice what you've learned.

TIP 3: Read every question carefully.

Make sure you understand each question before you choose your answer. Don't jump ahead and select an answer before you've read the entire question and *all* the answer choices.

 ## TIP 4: Go back and skim the passage for the correct answer.

To **skim** means to run your eyes quickly over a page. Skimming is an important reading skill, but you need to know when to use it. When taking a reading test, never skim instead of reading a passage from start to finish. *After* you've read the entire passage, however, the best way to find an answer is often to skim the passage for key words from the question.

TIP 5: Choose the best answer to the question.

Several of the answer choices may look good, but one will always be better than the rest. Make sure your choice is the *best* answer to the question being asked.

 TIP 6: Base your answers only on what is in the passage.

You're being tested on how well you read, not on how much outside knowledge you have about the topic of the passage. Every correct answer will be based on something stated in or supported by the passage. You can go back and look at the passage as much as you like.

 TIP 7: Don't let difficult questions freak you out.

Some questions may seem very difficult, but others will seem easy. If you come to a hard question, don't get too worried or upset. Just do your best to answer the question, then move on. A much easier question might be right around the corner.

 TIP 8: Don't leave any blanks.

Even if you aren't sure of an answer, always make your best guess. By answering, you at least have a chance to get the question right. Not answering is a sure way to miss.

Before you guess, always eliminate choices that seem as if they might be wrong. This will help you increase your odds of answering correctly.

 TIP 9: When it's time to take a test, relax.

Most people get a few butterflies in their stomachs when they have to take a test. It's normal. If you've practiced the material in this book, though, your reading skills will be "built-in" by test day. You won't need to worry because you'll know that you can do your best.

The Basics

Think of a friend you know well. Do you remember when you first met? You may have noticed a few basic things in that first meeting. Maybe you noticed that your friend smiled a lot, had curly red hair, or spoke with a quiet voice.

As you got to know your friend better, your friendship went deeper. You learned more about your friend's favorite foods, songs, and movies. Maybe you learned that your friend came from a large family, loved playing the piano, or had a pet flying squirrel.

Reading can be like getting to know a good friend. At first, you might notice a few basic things about a passage. You notice what it is mostly about, what the important details are, and so on. Later, you can get to know the passage— and the author—better.

In this unit, you will practice a few basic reading skills that will help you begin to "get acquainted" with a reading passage. In Units 2 and 3, you will learn how to gain a deeper understanding of the things you read.

In This Unit

Topic, Main Idea, and Theme

Supporting Details

Vocabulary

Reading and Study Strategies

Lesson 1: Topic, Main Idea, and Theme

Imagine you have just read a book called *The Mystery of Mortwitch Mansion*. A friend asks you, "So, what's it about?" You could answer this question in one of several ways.

You could tell your friend that the book is about a haunted house. This is the book's **topic**.

If you wanted to give your friend a little more information, you could say, "It's about two friends who decide to stay overnight in a haunted house and, when they do, they learn the real story about the house." This is the main idea of the book. The **main idea** is what a book or passage is mostly about. It is what the writer says *about* the topic.

Maybe you want to tell your friend what you learned from reading the book, so you say that the book is about how things aren't always what they seem to be. The **theme** is the message or lesson the author wants to share.

Novels aren't the only type of writing that have a topic, main idea, and theme. Plays, poems, short stories, and nonfiction writing all have them, too. In this lesson, you'll practice finding the topic, main idea, and theme of a reading passage.

Read the following passage. It will help you understand the tips in this lesson.

Kids Making a Difference
by Greta Anderson

You're only one person. On top of that, you're a kid. What can you do to help make the world a better place? In 1989, nine-year-old Melissa Poe of Nashville, Tennessee, faced the same problem. Concerned about the environment, Melissa began writing letters to the people in charge, starting with the president of the United States. When he didn't write back, Melissa only became more determined to be heard.

With five friends, Melissa started a club called Kids for a Clean Environment, or Kids F.A.C.E. They worked to get free billboard space to advertise their message. They also wrote to the media, and Melissa was soon asked to be a guest on the *Today* show. Other kids heard about the club, and more Kids F.A.C.E. club chapters started popping up around the world.

Today, Kids F.A.C.E. is the world's largest youth environmental organization, with more than 300,000 members in 23 countries. Members take part in such activities as planting trees, recycling, and preserving wildlife habitats.

Melissa Poe

Melissa has won several awards for her work. She was asked to speak at the Earth Summit in Brazil and has also attended special meetings with national and world leaders.

Keema McAdoo of Boston, Massachusetts, is another young person who has made a difference. As a middle-school student, she looked around and saw that many young people in her community were on drugs and hanging out in gangs. Worried about what might happen to her four younger sisters, Keema decided to help fight these problems. Luckily, there was an after-school outreach program she could join.

She found out that one reason kids in her neighborhood got into trouble was that they didn't have many positive activities to get involved in. Keema started "pick-up" basketball games and planned field trips to bowling alleys and ski areas. Soon, many kids in her neighborhood were having fun and avoiding dangerous activities.

When she grew older, Keema started a similar program at her high school. She and six friends also set up after-school activities at a nearby elementary school. They helped students with their schoolwork and even bought their own supplies, including books, crayons, and snacks. Most of all, they gave students the smiles and attention all kids need.

Like Melissa, Keema became someone people listened to. She spoke at important events and helped other schools start after-school programs. It isn't easy to speak out against the *status quo*,[1] but Keema had "the courage of her conviction." She knew that drugs and gangs are too dangerous for anyone to mess with.

[1] **status quo:** the way things are

So, what can *you* do? In every community, people your age have found ways to make a difference. Think about what message your community needs to hear or just what needs to be done. Talk about it with your friends to see what they think. Then, write letters to your community's leaders and to the editor of your newspaper.

Sometimes it's easiest to work with programs that already exist. There may be clubs in your area to join, such as the 4-H Club or other service organizations. Look around; you might be surprised at what you find. If there's no program to join, you can start one, as Melissa and Keema did. You might have to forge ahead on your own, but if you lead, others will follow.

Other Kids Leading the Way

When **Jason Crowe** of Newburgh, Indiana, lost his grandmother to cancer, he started a kids' newspaper, *The Informer*, in her memory. The newspaper contains stories about young people, and it addresses important issues such as pollution. Today, Jason's newspaper is read in 29 states.

Michael Wiener was upset when he saw a mother in a restaurant smoking next to her baby, surrounding the child with a cloud of smoke. As a result, he proposed a law to make restaurants seat children in nonsmoking areas. His law was first passed in Palm Desert, California, his hometown, and was later made into a state law.

Jena Sims of Winder, Georgia, began raising money to fight cancer when she was 10 years old. By the time she was 14, she had led 25 events to raise money. At 16, she began leading teams of runners in charity races. She now teaches others how to be team leaders.

 TIP 1: The topic of a passage can be stated in a word or a phrase.

The **topic** is the subject of a piece of writing. A topic should only be a couple of words, such as "birds," "trains," or "my summer vacation." You might be able to figure out the topic of a passage just by looking at the title. For example, if a passage is called "Rocks and Minerals of Vermont," it is probably going to be about the kinds of rocks and minerals found in Vermont.

If the title doesn't give it away, you can usually figure out the topic after you read only a few paragraphs or pages. If the passage about rocks in Vermont were called "Digging Up Vermont," you might not figure out the topic until you begin reading.

Once you think you've figured out the topic, make sure it isn't too broad or too narrow. The topic should be connected to the entire passage, not just part of it.

1. What is the main topic of the passage you just read?

    A. doing good

    B. thinking about problems

    C. speaking in public

    D. winning awards

 TIP 2: The main idea summarizes what the passage says about the topic.

The **main idea** of a passage is what a passage is mostly about. You can usually say the main idea in just once sentence.

Sometimes the author directly states the main idea in the passage. For example, in the passage about rocks in Vermont, you might find the main idea in the very first paragraph if the author states that "collectors can find many kinds of rocks and minerals in Vermont."

2. Go back to "Kids Making a Difference," and underline any sentences that tell the main idea.

 TIP 3: Think about how you would describe the passage to a friend.

Some passages come right out and tell you the main idea. Other passages give a lot of details. Details are small parts of the main idea. Think of details like pieces of a puzzle that come together to make a large picture. Details work together to create the main idea.

If the main idea is not directly stated, you will need to figure it out on your own. One way to do this is to summarize the passage in your mind. To **summarize** is to connect the most important parts of the passage together in one or two sentences. You don't need to repeat all of the details. Just hit the high points of the passage.

For example, imagine the passage about rocks in Vermont did not have a sentence telling you the main idea. Instead, it began by listing the tools you would need to become a rock collector. In the next paragraph, it described one type of rock you could collect in Vermont, and how to find it. The next paragraph described another rock, and so on.

To summarize the passage, you would need to connect all of those parts. But you don't want to just repeat all of the passage's details. Your summary might be something like this: "Rock collecting is a fun hobby, and with the right tools, collectors can find many kinds of rocks in Vermont."

Also be sure that your summary is not too broad. Imagine you have a friend named Calvin who says he doesn't like to read. You think he might enjoy reading "Kids Making a Difference," but you know it will take some convincing to get him to read it. If you tell him something like, "It's a great article about kids doing stuff," Calvin might give you a "Yeah, so what?" look. You'll need to be more specific.

3. Write a sentence summarizing "Kids Making a Difference."

_____

_____

_____

4. What is the main idea of this passage?

   A. Keema McAdoo started after-school activities for kids.

   B. Melissa Poe started an environmental club called Kids F.A.C.E.

   C. Kids are finding it difficult to make a difference in the world.

   D. Kids are leading others to improve their communities and the world.

Which choice would be the best way to summarize the article for Calvin? Think about the main point that connects all the information in the article. Then pick the choice that best sums up the *whole* passage.

 TIP 4: Know the difference between main idea and details.

Main idea questions often include wrong answer choices that are simply details from the passage. Remember, just because a statement is true doesn't mean it's the *main* idea. If a choice is mentioned only once in the passage, it's probably not the main idea. The main idea will be supported by nearly every paragraph in at least some small way.

For example, let's go back to our book about rocks in Vermont. Wrong answer choices might be about tools for rock collecting, one kind of rock you can collect in Vermont, or another fact from the passage. But all of these are just details. The main idea is what connects the details together.

5. Look at Number 4 again. Which choices are only details from the passage?

_____

 TIP 5: Main idea questions can be asked in different ways.

Not all main idea questions include the words *main idea*. Instead, some questions ask about the main idea in other ways. Some questions ask about the "central idea," or what the passage is "mostly about." Another question might ask you to choose a different title for the passage. Others ask you to choose a title or heading for only one part of the passage. Some ask you to pick the central idea of a paragraph or sidebar. A **sidebar** is a short fact or list of facts about the topic, usually in a box connected to the passage.

Answer the following questions about "Kids Making a Difference."

6. Which of the following would be a good title for this passage?

    A. You're Just a Kid
    B. Helping Kids Say "No" to Drugs
    C. How to Win Awards
    D. Making the World a Better Place

7. Which heading would be best for the first four paragraphs of this passage?

    A. Looking Out for Each Other
    B. Writing to Your Newspaper
    C. Protecting the Environment
    D. Changing the Laws

8. What is the central idea of the sidebar titled "Other Kids Leading the Way"?

    A. Michael Wiener proposed a law that was passed in his hometown.
    B. Jason Crowe and Jena Sims raised a lot of money to fight cancer.
    C. Crowe, Sims, and Wiener are three more examples of kids making a difference.
    D. Crowe, Sims, and Wiener all want to stop air pollution in their hometowns.

TIP 6: The theme of a passage is its basic message or lesson.

The **theme** is the message or lesson the author wants to share. A theme can be found in many different passages or stories while a main idea is special to one passage or book. A theme might be about dolphins, but the main idea would be something *about* dolphins like how smart they are. Some examples of themes are living in poverty, what it means to be an American, and becoming an adult. Once you figure out the theme, you can see how the whole piece of writing works together to present that message.

The more you read, the more you will notice themes that come up again and again. For example, many stories deal with the importance of friendship. You might read about the importance of friendship in a German fairy tale, a South American play, an African folktale, or a Native American fable. A **universal theme** is a theme that is the same for people all over the world.

Here are a few ways in which you might be asked about the theme of a passage:

- What is the theme of this passage?
- What would be a good motto for this passage?
- What is the main lesson this passage teaches?
- Which line from the passage best states the author's theme?

Answer the following questions about "Kids Making a Difference."

9. Which of the following best states the main theme of "Kids Making a Difference"?

   A. If you accomplish something great, people will listen to your ideas.

   B. Even young people can make a positive change in the world.

   C. There are many problems that need solving in the world.

   D. If you stay away from drugs and gangs, you will do better in school.

10. How do you know the answer to Number 9?

_____

_____

_____

TIP 7: The most important details are the ones that help explain the main idea or theme.

On your first read, figure out the main idea and theme of the passage. This will help you decide which details you should pay special attention to. The most important details are the ones that help explain the main idea or theme.

11. Which detail is most important to the main idea of "Kids Making a Difference"?

   A. Melissa started writing letters to the people.

   B. Keema has four younger sisters.

   C. Keema was asked to speak at important events.

   D. Michael Wiener is from Palm Desert, California.

 TIP 8: Scan the passage to find key words from the question.

To **scan** means to look quickly over the passage for something. One way to answer detail questions is to scan the passage for important words from the question. For example, look at the following question, but don't try to answer it yet.

   Why did Keema start pick-up basketball games?

Circle any words in the question above that might help you locate the answer in the passage. Then go back and find those words in the passage. Circle them each time they appear in the passage until you find the answer to the question.

Let's take another look at the question, this time with the answer choices.

12. Why did Keema start pick-up basketball games?

   A. because she wanted to become someone people listened to

   B. because kids needed positive activities to get involved in

   C. because she needed to raise money to buy phonics books

   D. because girls were not allowed to play on teams

Reading Practice

Directions: Read the passage and answer the questions that follow.

Big Feet

a Cherokee tale retold by Rick Zollo

This story took place a long time ago, when the world was young and the Great Creator had only just finished the job.

One of the creations was a bird, the meadowlark. Some of you might know the bird because it sings a most beautiful song. But way back when the world was new, this meadowlark would not sing. Such a sad bird, and you know why? Because its feet were so big.

Yes, that first meadowlark was ashamed. It would not sing or fly. Instead, it hid in the tall grass, sad that the Creator had given it such awful-looking feet.

One day, Grasshopper was skipping through the tall grass and came upon the meadowlark.

"What are you doing here, hiding? You should be living in trees, Meadowlark, and singing to the sky."

"It's my feet, Grasshopper. The Creator cursed me with these terrible gargantuan feet."

Grasshopper looked at Meadowlark's feet. Sure enough, they were big. "I will admit they are rather large. But do they stop you from flying? Do they prevent you from singing your song? Begone, I say. Act like a bird!"

Meadowlark took Grasshopper's advice and flew to the tallest tree. There Meadowlark could look out upon creation. The world looked so magnificent from such a perch that Meadowlark began to sing. Such a wonderful song with notes so clean and clear, you would think the Great Creator had placed this bird atop creation just to sing life's sweet song.

One by one, all the animals, even other birds, gathered 'round to hear Meadowlark's beautiful song. But once Meadowlark noticed the other animals, the bird was terribly embarrassed. *They are staring at my ugly feet*, thought this sad creature, and off it flew to hide again in the tall grass.

It just so happened that nearby a wheat field was ready for harvest. Living in this wheat field was Mother Quail, sitting on her nest of eggs. Grasshopper came upon the Quail, who was crying.

"They are coming to harvest the wheat, and my eggs have yet to hatch," cried the Quail.

Grasshopper had an idea. He went and found the sad Meadowlark. "I think we have a need for your big feet," said Grasshopper.

Grasshopper brought Meadowlark to the wheat field just as the Humans were getting ready to cut down their crop. Meadowlark used its enormous feet to carefully lift Quail's eggs and fly them to safety in the tall grass, where Quail was able to make another nest.

Quail's eggs were hatched in the very grass where Meadowlark once hid. And Meadowlark had to admit, "My feet are big, but they are good for something. I should not be so ashamed."

Ever since then, meadowlarks have proudly sung their songs.

1. What is the main idea of this passage?

   A. Meadowlark hides in the tall grass, afraid to let anyone see its big feet.

   B. Grasshopper finally gets Meadowlark to sing for the first time.

   C. Meadowlark's song is one of the most beautiful in nature.

   D. Meadowlark is ashamed of its big feet until it discovers they can be useful.

2. Which of the following would be the best new title for this passage?

   A. Why the Meadowlark Hides in the Tall Grass

   B. Grasshopper Saves Quail and Her Nest

   C. Meadowlark Learns to Be Proud

   D. Why the Meadowlark Does Not Sing

3. Which of the following best states the main theme of this passage?

   A. For every thing there is a purpose.

   B. Birds of a feather flock together.

   C. The early bird gets the worm.

   D. One good turn deserves another.

4. What is the main idea of the second paragraph of the passage?

   A. The first meadowlark was ashamed of its huge feet.

   B. The first meadowlark loved to sing about its huge feet.

   C. The first meadowlark had a beautiful singing voice.

   D. The first meadowlark was too sad about its big feet to sing.

5. Which of the following details best supports the main idea of the passage?

   A. Meadowlark flew to the tallest tree.

   B. A nearby wheat field was ready for harvesting.

   C. Quail's eggs were not ready to hatch yet.

   D. Meadowlark used its big feet to lift Quail's eggs to safety.

6. Who had the idea for Meadowlark to lift Quail's eggs from the wheat field?

   A. Meadowlark

   B. Quail

   C. Grasshopper

   D. The Creator

7. What lesson does Grasshopper help Meadowlark to learn? Use details from the story to support your answer.

_____

_____

_____

_____

_____

_____

_____

_____

Lesson 2: Supporting Details

Picture a house without any walls. Hard to imagine, isn't it? Although the roof might be the most important part of a house, it still needs walls for support. Passages, like houses, need firm support for their main ideas.

Writers use details to make their ideas clearer for the reader. For example, nonfiction writers use details to help or explain the main idea. Fiction writers use details to help readers imagine a setting, character, or action.

Detail questions are often the easiest questions to answer. That's because everything you need to know is right there in the passage. The following tips will help you spot important details and answer questions about them.

 TIP 1: Read the entire passage first.

When you first read an article or story, read every word. You don't need to remember every detail. Just get the big picture: What is the main idea? How is the passage organized? Try to make a "mental map" of the passage as you read, getting a general idea of where things are located.

Practice this tip as you read the following story.

adapted from

The Great Sea-Serpent

by Hans Christian Anderson

There was a little fish—a salt-water fish—of good family. I don't recall the name; you will have to get that from the learned people. This little fish had eighteen hundred brothers and sisters, all as old as he. All were obliged to look out for themselves. Each did as it pleased; each made out its own story. Their world had the strangest creatures, some very horrid and big with great gaping mouths that could gulp down all the eighteen hundred brothers and sisters. But they did not think of that, for as yet none of them had been swallowed.

The small ones swam side by side, close together, as herring and mackerel do. One day as they were swimming their merriest in the water and thinking of nothing, there sank—from up above—right down through them—a long, heavy thing that looked as if it never would come to an end. It stretched out farther and farther, much farther than they could see.

All the little fishes, and the great ones too, from the surface of the sea to the bottom, were thrown into a panic. The great horrid thing sank deeper and deeper, and grew longer and longer, miles and miles long! The fishes and snails and everything that swims, or creeps, or is driven by the current, saw this fearful thing—this enormous thing that had come down on them!

What kind of sea-eel was it? How would it act? How might they defend themselves? There was confusion and commotion among the rightful occupants of the sea.

A good many lobsters and crabs were so frightened, they ran out of their excellent shells and were obliged to wait for new ones to grow back again.

In all this fright and confusion, the eighteen hundred brothers and sisters became separated, and they never met again, or ever knew each other after that. Only some ten remained in the same place, and so in a few hours they got over their first fright and began to be curious about the affair. They looked about them. They looked up; they looked down; and down there in the depths, they saw the fearful thing that had scared them. It was quite thin, but they did not know how thick it might be able to make itself, or how strong it was. It lay very quiet, but that might be part of its cunning.

"Let it lie! It does not come near us!" said the most cautious of the little fishes. But the smallest one of all would not give up trying to find out what the thing might be. It had come from up above, so it was up above that one could find out about it.

So they swam up to the surface. It was perfectly still. They met a dolphin there. The dolphin is a sprightly fellow that turns somersaults on the water, and it has eyes to see with, so it must've seen the thing and would know all about it. They asked him, but he'd only been thinking about his somersaults, and saw nothing. He had no answer for them, and only looked high and mighty.

Then they turned to ask a seal, which was just plunging in. The seal was more civil (even though it usually eats small fish, today it had already eaten, so it was quite polite).

"He is quite thin," said the small fishes.

"They have starved him," said the seal, "but he will soon come to himself and be his old size again. I suppose he is the great sea-serpent that men are so afraid of and talk so much about. I never saw him before, and never believed in a sea-serpent, but I do now." With that, down went the seal.

"We can swim down and see for ourselves," said the littlest fish.

At last they all came to the place where the telegraph cable lay. "There lies the fellow!" cried all the great fishes, and the littlest one with them. They saw the cable, the beginning and end of which vanished beyond the reaches of their eyes.

The cable lay without stirring.

"The thing is crafty," said the whale. "It waits to strike me in the stomach, and that is my weak point."

"The thing is longer than I am," the sea-eel said, "but it is not length that does anything. One must have skin, stomach, and flexibility to hold a place of distinction down here."

The sea cow explained to them that this terrible thing was only some invention from the men on dry land. "They want to get hold of us," she said. "That's all they live for. They stretch nets for us and come with bait on a hook to catch us. That thing there is some kind of big string which they think we are going to bite at. They are such stupids! We are not. Do not touch it and it will shrivel up and turn to dust and mud. Everything that comes from up there is full of cracks and breaks—good for nothing."

"Good for nothing!" said all the creatures in the sea, and they held fast to the sea cow's opinion so as to have an opinion. But the littlest fish had its own thoughts: *That exceedingly long, thin serpent is perhaps the most wonderful fish in the ocean.*

 TIP 2: Notice which details are important.

You'll find a lot of details in just about any passage you read. It's the details that come together to create the meaning of the passage. Not all details are equal, however. Some are more important than others. As you learned in Lesson 1, the most important details are the ones that help explain the main idea of the passage. These ideas are said to support the main idea.

To figure out which details are the most important, first identify the main idea, then see which details are most closely linked to it.

1. What is the main idea of *The Great Sea-Serpent*?

   _____

   _____

You've identified the main idea. Now answer the following question. Keep in mind that the most important detail will be the one that most clearly supports the main idea.

2. Which of the following details best supports the main idea of the passage?

    A. The little fish has eighteen hundred brothers and sisters.

    B. Some lobsters and crabs are so frightened that they run out of their shells.

    C. The dolphin is only interested in turning somersaults.

    D. The little fish suggests swimming down to find out more about the thing.

 TIP 3: Skim the passage to find key words from the question.

To answer a detail question, you will need to look in the passage for key words. **Key words** are words in a passage that help you find an answer. You can find key words by skimming. To **skim** means to quickly look over the passage.

3. Take a look at the following question. Circle any words that might help you find the answer in the passage.

    What about the thing causes the fish to panic?

4. Now go back and find the key words you circled in Number 3 in the passage. When you find them, underline them. Carefully reread the sentences in which the key words appear.

Okay, let's take another look at the question, this time with the answer choices.

5. What about the thing causes the fish to panic?

    A. They don't know what it is.

    B. It attacks them without warning.

    C. It is a fishing line that may catch them.

    D. It strikes them in their stomachs.

Some students try to answer reading questions just by skimming—without reading the passage first. Skimming can help, but it also can lead you straight to the wrong answer if you don't have the big picture first.

TIP 4: You may be asked to decide which detail is NOT in the passage.

This kind of question isn't really any harder, it just may take a little longer. Look in the passage for key words from each of the answer choices. Then carefully compare to see which choice is NOT supported in the passage. It is a good idea to circle the key words in the passage when you find them.

6. Which phrase is not used to describe the thing?

    A. "some invention from the men on dry land"

    B. "the great sea-serpent that men are so afraid of . . ."

    C. "a long, heavy thing that looked as if it would never come to an end"

    D. "a sprightly fellow that turns somersaults on the water . . ."

By skimming the passage, you can locate key words from each of the answer choices.

 TIP 5: Notice the order in which events happen in the passage.

Sometimes, to make a story more interesting, writers will describe events out of order. You can expect order-of-events questions to be fairly straightforward, but you'll still need to read carefully to be sure.

7. Which of the following happens first in the story?

    A. The whale says the thing tickled its back.

    B. The seal says the thing is most likely a great sea-serpent.

    C. The little fishes swim up to talk with the dolphin.

    D. The sea cow says the thing is man's invention.

To answer this one, you need to skim to find the detail that happens first in the story. You can make sure you haven't missed one of the details by circling them as you skim. After you have found all of the choices in the passage, choose the one that happens first.

Here are a few more detail questions about *The Great Sea-Serpent*. As you answer them, you may wish to underline or circle key words in the passage.

8. Which of the following best describes the littlest fish?

    A. curious

    B. angry

    C. cowardly

    D. excited

9. What is the thing that startles the fish?

  A. sea-eel
  B. telegraph cable
  C. fishing line
  D. sea-serpent

10. What was the fish's first reaction to the thing?

  A. fear
  B. anger
  C. excitement
  D. braveness

Reading Practice

Directions: Read the passage and answer the questions that follow.

Is Anyone Out There?

by Ted Remington and Richard Apollo

Movies and television shows about aliens, such as *Star Wars* and *Superman*, have always been popular. In fact, thousands of books, films, and television programs have tried to picture what beings from other planets might be like. But is any of this stuff for real? Does life actually exist on other planets, or are creatures from space just something we make up for the fun of it?

For centuries, human beings have wondered whether life might exist anywhere else beside Earth. It's only been in the last few decades, however, that we have found the tools to help us answer this question. Telescopes now exist that are powerful enough to detect planets moving around other stars. Only a few have been found so far, but we do know that planets have formed around some stars besides our sun.

Astronomers also use giant radio receivers called radio telescopes that let them listen to radio waves that reach Earth from space. Most of what radio astronomers hear comes from natural sources, but they hope one day to hear a signal that definitely comes from intelligent beings.

There is a reason astronomers are looking into deep space for intelligent life: We are almost positive that no intelligent life besides us exists in our solar system. No planet in our solar system, other than Earth, has conditions that would support complex life forms. Some scientists believe that primitive life forms may have developed on Mars at one time.

Scientists also hope to find simple life forms on some of the solar system's moons, many of which are covered with ice. In 2004, astronomers launched the Cassini probe to visit Saturn and its icy moons. One part of the Cassini mission is to see if the building blocks of life might exist on Titan, Saturn's largest moon. Astronomers plan to launch another probe in 2015 to investigate Jupiter's icy moons—Europa, Callisto, and Ganymede—for signs of life.

If we haven't found even simple life on other planets, why do astronomers still search for signs of intelligent life? They point out that we've been looking for only a short period of time. Even a few decades isn't a long time when it comes to searching the entire galaxy!

Another point has been made by a famous radio astronomer named Frank Drake. He says that even if intelligent life is very rare, there's still a good chance we'll find it sooner or later. For intelligent life to exist—and for us to find it—a lot of factors need to come together. First, it would require a star similar to our sun that has an Earth-like planet the right distance away from it. The planet would need to have just the right mix of chemicals to create life and have the right conditions for this life to develop into intelligent beings. Finally, these beings would have to create the right technology to communicate with other planets and survive long enough to send signals into space. Otherwise, we would never hear from them.

Drake points out, however, that if even one star in 10 million had a planet that met all of these requirements, there would still be 10,000 intelligent civilizations in our galaxy alone. But if there are so many out there, why haven't we found even one of them?

There are reasons to believe or disbelieve in life on other planets. On one hand, it seems unlikely that in the whole universe only Earth would have life. On the other hand, we haven't found strong evidence that life exists anywhere else. How important is it to keep looking for life beyond Earth? What do we have to gain? Is there anything to lose? Should we increase our search for intelligent life, or would it be better to spend the time and money on other things?

1. Which of the following details best supports the main idea of the passage?

   A. *Star Wars* is one example of a popular movie about aliens.

   B. For centuries, humans have wondered about life on other planets.

   C. Scientists now have tools that can help them search for intelligent life.

   D. The moons of Jupiter and Saturn have icy surfaces.

2. Which of the following is not mentioned as something scientists have done to find life beyond Earth?

   A. sent space probes to distant galaxies

   B. looked for planets going around other stars

   C. listened for signals with radio telescopes

   D. planned to send probes to the moons of other planets

3. Which of the following details from the passage is most important?

   A. Movies and television shows about aliens have always been popular.

   B. Some books try to describe what alien life might look like.

   C. Planets have formed around other stars besides our sun.

   D. Frank Drake is a famous radio astronomer.

4. According to the passage, which of the following is not a requirement for intelligent life to develop?

   A. an Earth-like planet

   B. certain chemicals needed for life

   C. a star similar to our Sun

   D. a frozen surface

5. According to astronomer Frank Drake, how many planets with intelligent life might be in our galaxy?

   A. dozens

   B. hundreds

   C. thousands

   D. millions

6. What is the main idea of this passage?

   A. Movies about aliens from other planets are not very realistic.

   B. There is no evidence of life on any other planet or moon in our solar system.

   C. More money should be spent to search for intelligent life beyond Earth.

   D. Scientists are trying to answer the question of whether life exists beyond Earth.

7. Describe three ways scientists are searching for signs of life in space. Use details from the passage to support your answer.

   _____

   _____

   _____

   _____

   _____

   _____

   _____

   _____

   _____

Lesson 3: Vocabulary

Legendary . . . Ration . . . Daunted . . . Grudging . . . Insignificant . . .

The English language is made up of hundreds of thousands of words. How will you ever learn them all? The very thought of trying to learn all those words might leave you *petrified* (turned to stone, unable to act).

Luckily, you don't have to memorize a dictionary in order to become a good reader. Even the best readers come across difficult words once in a while. When they do, they have a few tricks up their sleeves to help them figure out the meanings of those words. If none of their tricks work, then they go to a dictionary or other resource. In this way, the more they read, the more their vocabulary grows.

In this lesson, you will learn a few tricks to help you figure out the meanings of unfamiliar words. If you use these skills—along with a dictionary—in your everyday reading, soon you will have a gargantuan vocabulary. You'll also be ready for any multiple-choice vocabulary questions that come your way.

Read the following passage. It will be used to help you understand the tips in this lesson.

English: A Living Language
by Greta Anderson and Red Gomez

Do you know of a good history book? We do, and we'll bet you've already read some of it: the dictionary. The English language holds many tales of the island on which it was born. It also hints at the many cultures with which English speakers have mingled over the centuries. In many dictionaries, you can read the shorthand of these tales. In the word entries, brackets containing abbreviations such as *OE*, *Gk*, and *Sp*[1] tell where each word originated and give hints about how the word came to us today.

England—Where It All Began

For centuries (from 43 to 410 C.E., to be exact), Rome had control over England and over the Celtic people, who had lived there as long as anyone could remember. But England was far, far away from the government headquarters in Rome. The Romans built a few roads, towns, and army camps, but their Latin language was not heavily absorbed by the natives.

[1] **OE:** Old English; **Gk:** Greek; **Sp:** Spanish

When the Romans departed, however, they left the door wide open for other peoples to arrive and take over the island. Germanic tribes from Europe sailed across the North Sea looking for land and riches. In the face of these cruel invaders, the Celts scattered off to Wales and Ireland. England became the new home of the Germanic tribes, known as the Angles, the Saxons, and the Jutes.

The languages these tribes spoke gave us most of our basic words today. *A*, *and*, *the*, *is*, *have*, *go*, *see*, *get*, *to*, *for*, and *of* are all Anglo-Saxon words. In fact, most of our single-syllable words have German origins: *man*, *stink*, *breathe*, *work*, and *ground* are just a few. The Anglo-Saxons did not use the same letters we use, however. They wrote in **runes**, or pictures that symbolized words and ideas.

This is the rune *jera*, which coincides with the Roman letter *j* or *y* and means "season." (Guess where the word *year* came from.) The lines are meant to show rows of planting.

In the centuries that followed, Christian missionaries arrived on the island. The Anglo-Saxons eventually adopted the alphabet those missionaries used: the Roman alphabet, the same alphabet we use today.

In 1066, the Normans streamed across the English Channel to claim England as theirs. William the Conqueror and the rest of the Norman people spoke French, which at the time was very similar to Latin. They made their conquest complete by forcing anyone who dealt with them (mostly royals and wealthy landowners) to use the French language.

Of course, a lot goes on in society besides what happens in courts and castles. After the French soldiers congratulated themselves on a successful invasion, they began to look for wives. The women they found spoke Old English and liked that language just fine. So the men went on speaking French and the women went on speaking Old English, and eventually they understood each other. Middle English, a mix of words from French and English, was born. Because the French language came from Latin, Middle English also had a strong Latin influence.

In the mid-1400s, Johannes Gutenberg invented the printing press in Germany. Several years later, William Caxton brought the technology home to England. Once the English language was printed, the language began to be smoothed out and the spellings standardized.

American English—A Cultural Blend

Not long afterward came the Age of Exploration, and Europeans made their way to the Americas. The English, Spanish, Portuguese, French, and Dutch all tried to grab parts of this "New World." In the struggle that followed, the other nations lost control of most of North America to England, which soon dominated the area. English became the talk of the land.

When the English first arrived, many Native American nations lived on the vast continent. Many of their words, such as *chocolate*, *tomato*, and *potato*, and place-names such as *Massachusetts* and *Arkansas*, worked their way into the English vocabulary.

Slaves were brought over mostly from Africa, and they also added to the language. Words such as *gumbo* and *jazz* came from African languages. Much of today's music and fashions draw from African-American heritage, and with these new trends come new words.

Spanish influences can be heard in words such as *buffalo*, *ranch*, *barbecue*, and *California*. Spanish continues to affect English; the largest group of new U.S. citizens comes from Spanish-speaking lands.

America's melting pot has led to a language stew. The English language contains more than 600,000 words, and it's still growing. In fact, English has more words than many other languages. So many words, and each with a tale to tell.

Vocabulary in Context

As you learned in the passage, the English language is always changing and growing. It would be easier if all writing was made up of words with only one possible meaning. But words affect each other, and their meanings can change depending on what other words are nearby.

When you read, think of yourself as a "word detective." Whenever you come to an unknown word, you put on your detective hat, get out your magnifying glass, and look around for clues at the scene. These clues will give you hints about the meaning of the unknown word.

Of course, we don't expect you to wear a detective's hat when you read, although you can if you like. However, even without a hat, you can still be a word detective by looking for clues around any unknown words you find. What are these clues? Other words.

Where New Words Come From

New words enter our language all the time. Many come from other cultures as English-speaking people take part in the global economy. Technology also brings new terms into the language, such as *space station* and *website*. The business world sometimes coins new words, such as *proactive* (to be active in predicting and solving problems). Governments create terms to describe their activities, such as *shuttle diplomacy* (negotiations made by a person who "shuttles" back and forth between two countries).

To see how this works, read the following sentence.

> Getting ready for a sleepover at her cousin's house, Olivia packed her new <u>bizaflak</u>. She was amazed that it could hold not only a ton of clothes, but also a board game, her favorite pillow, and all her CDs.

You may not know what a *bizaflak* is, but the other words in the paragraph give you plenty of hints. You know a *bizaflak* is something that is packed before a sleepover. You know it holds clothes and lots of other items. Use these clues to answer the following question.

1. What is a bizaflak?

   A. a type of game

   B. a kind of travel bag

   C. a piece of clothing

   D. a kind of sleeping bag

See how easy it can be? (By the way, you won't find *bizaflak* in any dictionary. We made it up.)

Figuring out the meaning of a word by looking at the other words around it is called using **context**. Following are a few tips for using this important skill.

 TIP 1: Look in the passage for other words with a similar meaning.

Words that have similar meanings are called **synonyms**. When you encounter an unknown word in a passage, look for other words nearby that may be synonyms of the unknown word. This may help you figure out the meaning of the new word. For example, read the following sentence, then answer Numbers 2 and 3.

> Charlie is quite <u>ambitious</u>. He wants to do well in his chosen profession: politics.

2. Circle the word or phrase that has about the same meaning as *ambitious*.

3. As used in this sentence, what does the word *ambitious* mean?

   A. hope for ideas

   B. hope for speed

   C. hope for success

   D. hope for courage

4. Read the following sentence from "English: A Living Language."

When the Romans <u>departed</u>, however, they left the door wide open for other peoples to arrive and take over the island.

As it is used in this sentence, *departed* means that the Romans did which of the following?

A. left England

B. came to England

C. destroyed England

D. started at England

5. Read the following paragraph from the passage.

In 1066, the Normans streamed across the English Channel to claim England as theirs. William the Conqueror and the rest of the Norman people spoke French, which at the time was very similar to Latin. They made their <u>conquest</u> complete by forcing anyone who dealt with them (mostly royals and wealthy landowners) to use the French language.

What does the word *conquest* mean in this paragraph?

A. defeat

B. takeover

C. travels

D. learning

 TIP 2: Look for clues to the word's opposite meaning.

The sentence or paragraph in which the unknown word appears will sometimes give you clues to the meaning of the word. One clue is the word's antonym. An **antonym** is a word that means the *opposite* of another word. If you can figure out what a word's antonym is, then you will be able to make a good guess about its meaning.

Read the following sentence, then answer Numbers 6 and 7.

Despite Erica's serious tone, I found her story about trolls playing Frisbee on her lawn to be quite <u>hilarious</u>.

6. Circle a word in the sentence that means the opposite of *hilarious*.

7. What does *hilarious* mean?

    A. scary

    B. interesting

    C. untrue

    D. funny

8. Read the following sentences from the passage.

    > The English, Spanish, Portuguese, French, and Dutch all tried to grab parts of this "New World." In the struggle that followed, the other nations lost control of most of North America to England, which soon <u>dominated</u> the area.

    What does the word *dominated* mean?

    A. failed

    B. considered

    C. controlled

    D. overlooked

 TIP 3: Plug in each answer choice in place of the unknown word.

Another way to figure out the answer to a vocabulary question is to insert each choice in the place of the unknown word. The choice that fits best in the context of the passage is most likely the correct answer.

Try this tip on the following passage and question. (Don't answer the question yet.)

> The knights were <u>indignant</u>. What could this mere child know about slaying dragons and saving kingdoms? How dare this unworthy youngster challenge the best of them to a joust!

9. As it is used in the passage, what does *indignant* mean?

    A. insulted

    B. joyous

    C. saddened

    D. frightened

Even if you don't know exactly what *indignant* means, you can probably figure out the answer. Substitute each answer choice in place of the word *indignant* in the passage, as shown below.

A. The knights were <u>insulted</u>. What could this mere child know about slaying dragons and saving kingdoms? How dare this unworthy youngster challenge the best of them to a joust!

B. The knights were <u>joyous</u>. What could this mere child know about slaying dragons and saving kingdoms? How dare this unworthy youngster challenge the best of them to a joust!

C. The knights were <u>saddened</u>. What could this mere child know about slaying dragons and saving kingdoms? How dare this unworthy youngster challenge the best of them to a joust!

D. The knights were <u>frightened</u>. What could this mere child know about slaying dragons and saving kingdoms? How dare this unworthy youngster challenge the best of them to a joust!

Which answer choice makes the most sense when it is plugged into the passage? Go back to Number 9 and circle the correct answer.

Now use the plug-in method to answer the following question about "English: A Living Language."

10. Read these sentences from the passage "English: A Living Language."

> The English language holds many tales of the island on which it was born. It also hints at the many cultures with which English speakers have <u>mingled</u> over the centuries.

In the above paragraph, what does the word *mingled* mean?

A. fought

B. created

C. mixed

D. distanced

TIP 4: Don't be fooled by multiple-meaning words.

Homonyms are words that can have more than one meaning. Here is a short list of examples.

- *Pool* can mean a game, a body of water, or a place to swim.
- *Ball* can mean a round object or a fancy dance party.
- *Tick* can mean a kind of insect or the sound a clock makes.
- *Gross* can mean disgusting or a package of twelve dozen.
- *Bank* can mean the side of a river or a place to keep money.
- *Rock* can mean a lump of stone or to sway back and forth.
- *Top* can mean the highest point or a spinning toy.

When answering vocabulary questions, make sure you always go back to the reading passage to see how the word is used. Read the following passage, then answer Number 11.

Swoosh! The ball dropped straight through the <u>hoop</u>—no backboard, no rim, nothing but net.

11. In this passage, what is a hoop?

   A. a plastic toy that a person rotates around the hips
   B. a metal band used to hold together the boards in a barrel
   C. a metal ring through which a ball is thrown to score points in a basketball game
   D. one of two rings used to hold a piece of material in place, as in embroidery

The word *hoop* can mean many things. Which meaning best fits the context of the sentence?

12. Read the following lines from "English: A Living Language."

   Spanish influences can be heard in words such as *buffalo, ranch, barbecue,* and *California.* Spanish continues to <u>impact</u> English: The largest group of new U.S. citizens comes from Spanish-speaking lands.

What does the word *impact* mean in these lines?

   A. destroy completely
   B. hit with great speed
   C. force open
   D. have an effect on

The word *impact* has more than one meaning, too. Make sure you choose the correct meaning in the context of the passage. If you're still not sure, plugging in each answer choice can help you figure out which meaning of the word is the best fit.

Word Parts

As you learned in "English: A Living Language," many words in the English language come from other languages. English is called a Germanic language, and many of our small words come from German. However, over half of all English words actually come from Latin, because of the Norman invasion of England in 1066. The Normans spoke French, which grew out of Latin.

English words with Latin origins are often made up of smaller parts. The parts come from Latin words, and together they are assembled into new English words. These parts may include a root word and one or more prefixes or suffixes. When a prefix or suffix is attached to a root word, the meaning of the word changes. It may change a little or a lot. Knowing the meanings of some common word parts will help you figure out the meanings of many difficult words.

 TIP 5: A root forms the base of a word.

The **root** part of a word is the bottom or basic part of the word. Think of it as the simplest part of a word that has the most meaning.

Take the word *sunflower*. Half of the word *sunflower* is *sun*, and the other half is *flower*. If you just looked at *sun*, then you might think that a sunflower has something to do with the actual sun. However, if you look at the *flower* part of the word, you understand that a sunflower is a flower. So, *flower* is the root part of the word *sunflower* because *flower* tells you most of the meaning. The *sun* part of sunflower just tells you what type of flower it is: a big yellow flower that always faces the sun.

Here is a list of common roots you should know, along with some examples.

13. Look up the definition of each example in a dictionary, then write your own examples on the lines provided.

Root	Definition	Examples	
auto, aut	self	automatic, author	_____
bio	life	biography	_____
graph, gram	write	autograph, grammar	_____
hydr, hydra, hydro	water	dehydrate, hydroelectric	_____

Root	Definition	Examples	
micro	small	microscope	_____
sci	know	conscious	_____
scope	see	telescope	_____
zo, zoo	animal	zoology	_____

Now answer the following question about "English: A Living Language," keeping the idea of root words in mind.

14. What does the word *originated* mean in the first paragraph?

    A. started from

    B. ended up

    C. understood to mean

    D. allowed to happen

 TIP 6: Prefixes are added to the beginnings of root words.

A **prefix** is added to the beginning of a root word to change the root word's meaning. Look at the following example:

> *pre* (meaning "before") + *view* (see) = *preview* (to see before)

Here is the new word used in a sentence:

> After what happened last week, the principal asked to preview the daily list of announcements to be read over the intercom.

15. Following is a list of common prefixes you should know, along with some examples. Write your own examples on the lines provided.

Prefix	Definition	Examples	
ab-	away, off	abnormal, abuse	_____
dis-	the opposite of, the absence of	dislike, discourage	_____

Prefix	Definition	Examples	
im-	not, into	impatient, implant	_____
in-	the opposite of, not, into	injustice, inject	_____
mis-	bad, badly, wrongly, not	mistrust, misadventure	_____
non-	not, the opposite of	nonworking, nonsense	_____
over-	beyond, more than	overwork, overjoyed	_____
pre-	before	preheat, prehistoric	_____
un-	the opposite of, not	unlike, unblinking	_____
under-	less than, not enough, beneath, hidden	undercook, undercover	_____

Now answer the following question about "English: A Living Language."

16. Read this sentence from the passage.

> The Romans built a few roads, towns, and army camps, but their Latin language was not heavily <u>absorbed</u> by the natives.

What does *absorbed* mean?

A. let out

B. taken up

C. lifted up

D. given up

TIP 7: Suffixes are added to the ends of root words.

A **suffix** is added to the end of a root word to change the meaning of the root word. Look at the following example.

> hope + ful = hopeful *(full of hope)*

> Ty was <u>hopeful</u> that his school would once again win the basketball championship.

17. The following is a list of common suffixes you should know, along with some examples. Write your own examples on the lines provided.

Suffix	Definition	Examples	
-able	able or worthy to be or become something	workable, adorable	_____
-en	to make more so, made of	weaken, wooden	_____
-ful	full of, having a lot of	sorrowful, cheerful	_____
-ity	having the character or quality of, being a certain way	probability, reality	_____
-less	without or lacking something	cheerless, worthless	_____
-ly	in such a manner, like or suited to, happening every so often	partly, earthly, monthly	_____
-ness	the state of being something	mildness, tenderness	_____
-ology	the study of	zoology, biology	_____
-ous	full of or having something	marvelous, glamorous	_____
-ion, -sion, -tion	act of, state of, result of	celebration, tension	_____

Practice Activity

Directions: Complete each of the following by writing the new word and its meaning.

Prefix	Root	Suffix	New Word	New Meaning
1. im-	perfect		_____	_____
2. mis-	place		_____	_____
3.	glory	-ous	_____	_____
4.	skill	-ful	_____	_____
5.	rely	-able	_____	_____
6.	friend	-less	_____	_____
7. non-	perish	-able	_____	_____
8. dis-	respect	-ful -ly	_____	_____

 TIP 8: Learn new words wherever you find them.

The language arts aren't the only subjects in which to learn new words. You can pick up new vocabulary from almost all the things you read for school (and even in the things you read for fun).

In math class, for example, you might learn the word *median* (middle). In science, you might pick up the word *phenomenon* (an observable fact or event). And in social studies, you might come across the word *chicle* (an important crop in some South American countries, and the main ingredient in chewing gum).

TIP 9: Use your dictionary!

When you aren't sure about the meaning of a word, look it up in a dictionary. You may not remember every word you look up. Over time, however, you'll build a powerful vocabulary. (You won't be able to use a dictionary on most standardized tests, but use one as you practice anyway.) Dictionaries can also tell you how a word is pronounced, where it comes from, what part of speech it is, and examples of how it is used.

As you gain more practice with the tips in this lesson, you may find that you can figure out a lot about new words before you check the dictionary. Being a "word detective" can help you learn the patterns that make English a living language.

More Word Tools

Here are a few more tools to help you in your reading and writing.

glossary – gives meanings of words used in a certain book; often found in textbooks

thesaurus or **synonym finder** – lists words with similar meanings

spell-check program – locates spelling errors in electronic documents and makes suggestions for correcting them; usually part of a word-processing program

Reading Practice

Directions: Read the passage and answer the questions that follow.

John Muir

by Dan Duncalf

"Climb the mountains and get their good tidings. Nature's peace will flow into you as sunshine flows into trees. The winds will blow their own freshness into you, and the storms their energy, while cares will drop off like autumn leaves."

—John Muir

John Muir wrote that the hope of the world was in the wilderness. He loved the outdoors so much that he spent most of his life working to save it from development.

Muir was born in Scotland in 1838. When he was 11 years old, his family moved to the United States. They lived on a farm in Wisconsin. John worked hard on the farm and didn't have much time for school. He loved books, however, so he studied on his own.

As a teenager, John was an inventor. He invented a large outdoor thermometer and an automatic horse feeder. His inventions won a prize at the state fair. Because of his success, he was admitted to the University of Wisconsin.

John Muir

After college, John Muir took a job in a machine shop. One day, a piece of metal went into his eye, causing him to be temporarily blind. While he was recovering in the hospital, he decided he would never work in a factory again.

When he was well, Muir began to travel. First he walked a thousand miles from Indiana to Florida. Then he took a ship to Cuba. After Cuba, he traveled first to New York, and finally to California. He spent the next five years hiking in the mountains. He camped alone for weeks at a time with just his blanket roll and a little food. As he learned about the Sierra Nevada mountains, he fell deeply in love with them and decided to dedicate his life to their preservation.

A few years later, he began to give speeches. His audiences were often spellbound as he described the wonders of the wilderness. He also wrote magazine articles about these wonders. Through these articles, the American people began to understand why it was important to save forests and mountain meadows from being developed. Largely because of John Muir, the U.S. Congress set aside millions of acres of beautiful wilderness for all Americans to enjoy.

1. Read this sentence from the passage.

   One day, a piece of metal went into his eye, causing him to be <u>temporarily blind</u>.

   What do the words *temporarily blind* mean?

   A. to be blind permanently
   B. to have increasing blindness
   C. to have continuing blindness
   D. to be blind for a limited time

2. Read these sentences from the passage.

   After college, John Muir took a job in a machine shop. One day, a piece of metal went into his eye, causing him to be temporarily blind. While he was <u>recovering</u> in the hospital, he decided he would never work in a factory again.

   What does the word *recovering* mean?

   A. becoming sick
   B. remembering back
   C. thinking about one's life
   D. getting one's health back

3. Read this sentence from the passage.

> As he learned about the Sierra Nevada mountains, he fell deeply in love with them and decided to <u>dedicate</u> his life to their preservation.

What does the word *dedicate* mean?

A. worship
B. devote
C. honor
D. work

4. What is this passage mainly about?

A. John Muir's love for the outdoors
B. the inventions of John Muir
C. the mountains of California
D. John Muir's accidental eye injury

5. Which of the following did John Muir do first?

A. work in a machine shop
B. write magazine articles
C. hike in the mountains
D. walk from Indiana to Florida

6. Where did John Muir receive his eye injury?

A. in Scotland
B. in a factory
C. in the mountains
D. in college

7. Why did John Muir spend his life trying to preserve the wilderness? Support your answer with details from the passage.

_____

_____

_____

_____

_____

_____

_____

_____

_____

Lesson 4: Reading and Study Strategies

Every good team goes into a game with a plan, a strategy. Before every basketball game, the players warm up. They must get their muscles ready to work and their minds ready for the mental challenge. During the game, the strategy may simply be to give the ball to Samir, or for each player to guard a player on the other team. After the game, the strategy may include reviewing the game, and deciding what was most difficult, in order to know how to practice for the next game.

The same thing is true of reading. Your reading strategy should include a plan for what to do before, during, and after you read. When you are reading, you can have a plan for attacking the page, section, chapter, or book. This lesson will give you some basic ways to get more from your reading.

Read the following passage. It will help you understand the tips in this lesson.

Know the Yo!

by Steven Ramirez

Walk the Dog. Hop the Fence. Loop the Loop. Eat Spaghetti. What do all of these have in common? They are all names of popular yo-yo tricks! While these tricks may be new, the yo-yo happens to be the second oldest toy in the world (next to the doll). Some people today even see the yo-yo as much more than a toy. They see it as a challenging sport. Every year, in countries such as the U.S., Brazil, Mexico, and Japan, professional yo-yoers compete in yo-yo championships to see who can do the most tricks.

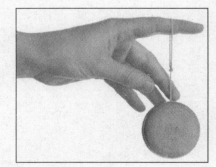

From Tool to Toy

The toy that we call the "yo-yo" is actually 2,500 years old. Pictures of this toy can be seen on the walls of Egyptian temples. Museums still have the clay yo-yos that ancient Greeks gave to their children as gifts. Some believe that before the yo-yo was used as a toy in Egypt and Greece, it was used as a hunting tool in the Philippines. Natives would tie a sharp rock to the end of a long rope. They would then wait in trees for animals to pass by and, when they did, the hunters would release their rocks, hit their target, and pull the rock right back up.

When the yo-yo was brought to Europe, hundreds of years later, it wasn't seen as a hunting tool anymore. It was seen as a great idea for a toy. Instead of rope, people began to tie rubber bands to smaller stones so that it could return to their fingers easily and without hurting anyone. This little toy became so popular that kings and queens could be seen playing with their own fancier versions. Napoleon Bonaparte, the famous war general during the French Revolution, even owned a few of these toys and played with them often. It didn't have a name yet, but it was a sensation!

The Yo-Yo in America

In the 1920s, a man named Pedro Flores decided to open up a store in America that sold these toys. But what was it to be called? Pedro was originally from the Philippines and he happened to know the history of the toy. He decided the best thing to do would be to use a word from the Filipino language. He came up with "yo-yo," which means "come, come" or "return." Soon, Pedro's Yo-Yo Manufacturing Company was making over 300,000 yo-yos a day. Pedro's yo-yos were made from a single block of wood and a thin string, which made it more comfortable to use and easier to carry.

One day, a man named Donald Duncan saw Pedro's yo-yo. He knew he could make the toy even more popular that it already was. So Donald bought Pedro's company for 250,000 dollars. Soon after, Donald invented the loop slip-string. Thanks to this type of loose knot, the yo-yo was able to spin faster at the end of the string and for a longer time. With the help of television commercials, the yo-yo craze spread across America. Donald sold them in different colors, designs, and sizes. He created yo-yo competitions and watched as kids from all over discovered new tricks. The yo-yo had arrived.

A New Sport

Today, the World Yo-Yo Contest is held in Florida during the summer months. This contest brings in yo-yo champions from all over the world to compete against each other. People of all ages stand on a stage and "freestyle" their yo-yo skills to music in front of a panel of judges. Sometimes, these yo-yoists will use two and three yo-yos at one time.

Even if you don't know how to master such tricks as the Atom Smasher, the Forward Pass, Texas Star, or the Cyclone Racer, you can still spend hours with the yo-yo. It may not take batteries, it may not use control sticks, and it may not make much noise, but the yo-yo continues to be one of the world's oldest and most popular toys.

TIP 1: First, know what you are reading.

Before you begin reading, preview the passage. This will provide you with a lot of information about the passage before you really get into it. Then you can make a few predictions about what you expect the passage will be about. To **predict** means to guess what is going to happen. Predictions should always be based on information, not just on wild guesses.

First, take a glance at the passage to get a rough idea of what it's about. You can gather a lot of information simply by doing the following:

- Look at the **title**.

- Read the **introduction**, if there is one.

- Look at any **headings**, **subheadings**, **boxed text** or **sidebars**, and any words in **boldface** or *italic print*.

- Look at any **pictures**, **diagrams**, or other **illustrations**.

Next, figure out what type of passage you are about to read. A **genre** is a type of writing. If you are able to identify the passage's genre, you'll have a better idea of how to approach the passage. Most writing falls into one of the following categories:

Fiction tells a made-up story. These are some examples of fictional stories:

- **contemporary fiction** – stories that take place in today's world

- **science fiction** – fantasy stories that involve science topics or the future

- **historical fiction** – stories loosely based on events from history

- **myth** – a traditional story that attempts to explain the beliefs and surroundings of a culture

- **legend** – a short story about past events, often including unearthly elements

- **fairy tale** – a type of folktale, usually written for children and often featuring unearthly characters

- **folktale** – a story from a group of people or region, originally passed on through oral tradition

- **fable** – a type of folktale, often with animal characters, that provide moral lessons

Nonfiction tells about real-life people, places, things, events, or ideas. The following are some examples of nonfiction:

- **autobiography** – the story of a person's life, written by that person

- **biography** – the story of a person's life, written by someone other than that person

- **diary (or journal)** – written record of the events and experiences of a person's life

- **essay** – writing that examines a topic or expresses an idea

- **editorials** – columns often written by experts or "insiders" attempting to persuade readers to agree with an idea or take an action. Editorials tend to base their arguments on both facts and opinions and are usually about social topics.

- **instructions** – directions that teach how to perform a task

Drama is written to be performed by actors. The script of a play tells the actors which lines to speak, and most of the plot is usually revealed through the characters' words. The two main types of drama are tragedy and comedy.

Poetry comes in all styles, shapes, and sizes. Some poems tell a story; others simply describe an image. Some rhyme; others don't. All poems use language in a special or memorable way.

Look again at the passage "Know the Yo!" as if you are previewing it. Then answer Numbers 1 through 4.

1. What type of passage is it? (Circle the correct answer.)

   Fiction   Nonfiction   Poetry   Drama

2. What is the passage about?

   _____

3. What kinds of things do you expect to learn from the passage?

   _____

   _____

   _____

4. Which of the following questions do you think the passage will most likely answer?

    A. Where did the yo-yo come from?

    B. How do I do yo-yo tricks?

    C. How do I make my own yo-yo?

    D. How much money does it cost to buy a yo-yo?

As you read a passage, you will find out whether your predictions are right or wrong. Either way, making predictions helps your mind get involved in the passage and know a little bit about what to expect.

 TIP 2: Remind yourself of what you already know about the topic.

Another way to warm up is to recall what you already know about the topic. Your own knowledge and experiences are your best guide to understanding what you read. Also, ask yourself what you might like to learn about the topic.

You can use a K-W-L chart like the one on the following page to record your thoughts. **K-W-L** stands for Know, Want to Know, and Learned. In the left-hand column, jot down what you already **Know** (K) about the topic before reading the passage, chapter, or book. In the center column, write what you **Want to Know** (W)—any questions you would like to explore about the topic. You will come back to the chart and use the right-hand column to record what you've **Learned** (L) later in this lesson.

Know the Yo!

What I Know	What I Want to Know	What I Learned
a yo-yo is a small toy it goes up and down a string	Why is a yo-yo called a yo-yo?	

TIP 3: Match your strategy to the type of passage you are reading and your reasons for reading it.

You read in different ways depending on what you are reading and why. For example, when you use a phone book, you quickly skim through the text until you find the name and number you need. When reading a textbook for school, you read slowly and carefully, perhaps making notes of important facts you'll need to remember.

The following are a few reading strategies you might choose, depending on your task.

- **Previewing** involves looking over a passage to get an idea of what it contains and how it is organized.

- **Careful reading** requires you to read every word of the passage in order to understand the main ideas and important supporting details. Understanding the text is far more important than speed.

- **Rereading** parts of a passage helps you understand it better. Rereading also helps if you come across an important point and want to firmly plant it in your mind. Perhaps you want to reread the text simply because you enjoy it.

- **Skimming** involves running your eyes over the passage, looking for something specific. When answering test questions, you might skim a passage for key words from the question, as described in Lesson 2. This helps you focus on the parts of the passage that are most related to the question.

> ### Many Readers, Many Reasons to Read
>
> There are many reasons to read. A few are listed below. Can you think of others?
>
> - to be entertained
> - to learn
> - to appreciate the writer's craft
> - to get ideas for your own writing
> - to write a response
> - to do everyday tasks, such as completing forms and responding to letters
> - to find information
> - to solve problems
> - to help others about a topic

In other lessons of this book, you will learn more specific strategies for reading certain types of passages, such as poetry and instructions.

TIP 4: **To keep your mind active, keep your pencil moving.**

Reading isn't just a matter of soaking up words as they pass before your eyes. It requires getting your mind involved with the ideas the author is presenting. One good way to keep your mind working is to make notes. Here are a few suggestions:

- Underline important ideas.

- Circle new vocabulary words to look up later.

- In the margins, jot down one or two words that tell what a paragraph is about.

- Do you find part of the passage difficult to understand? If so, mark it and come back later.

- Does the passage remind you of an experience you've had? Make a note of it.

Don't worry too much about whether you are marking the "right" information in the passage. The important thing is to keep your mind involved. Writing down questions, thoughts, understandings, and connections will keep your mind alert and awake.

⚠ You probably aren't allowed to write in your textbooks or in library materials. In these cases, make notes about the passage on a separate sheet of paper. When taking some standardized tests, you might not be allowed to write in your test booklet.

5. Go back to the passage "Know the Yo!" Underline the most important parts. Circle any new vocabulary. Make notes in the margins with your thoughts about the passage.

TIP 5: Notice how the passage is organized.

To **organize** means to put in some sort of order. You can organize many things like a desk, a room, your thoughts, or a passage. Authors can organize nonfiction articles in many ways. Some examples are in the sidebar "Nonfiction Structures." As you read, notice how the passage is structured. This will help you know what to expect and where in the passage to return for specific information. Sketching a quick graphic organizer can help you follow the organization of the passage. Here are a few examples of graphic organizers:

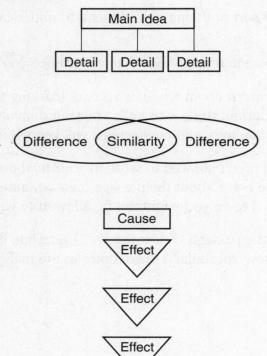

Nonfiction Structures

Here are a few basic nonfiction organizational structures:

• cause and effect

• chronological order (in order by time)

• comparison and contrast

• description

• main idea and supporting details

• stages of a process

• moving from a general idea to specific ideas

• moving from specific ideas to a general idea

6. Complete the following graphic organizer by filling in the blanks.

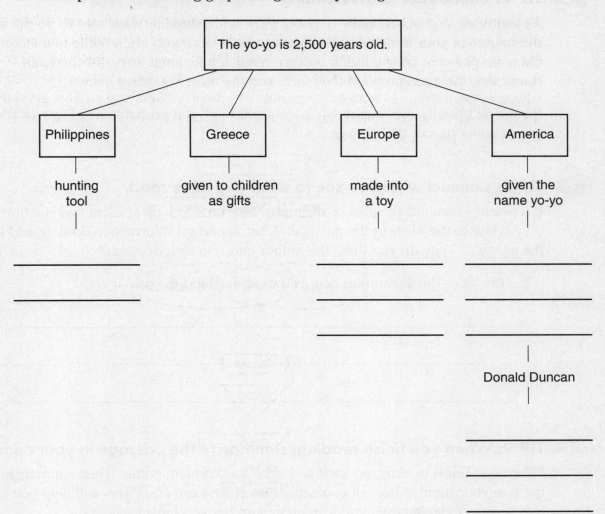

The yo-yo is 2,500 years old.

| Philippines | Greece | Europe | America |

hunting tool

given to children as gifts

made into a toy

given the name yo-yo

Donald Duncan

 TIP 6: Continue to ask questions and to make connections and predictions.

The passage may cause new questions to come to your mind. Use your K-W-L chart to list new questions, or write them in the margins next to the passage. You may simply want to keep your questions in mind as you continue to read. One way to help yourself think about the passage is to ask questions that begin with *who, what, when, where, why,* or *how.*

An important question to ask is, *Where is this passage going?* Using clues from a passage to guess what's going to happen later is called **predicting.** Continue to make predictions about what will come next in the passage. Also, continue to connect the passage to your own knowledge and experiences, and to other things you have read. To **connect** means to find how ideas and events join together in different ways. Think about how the ideas in the passage relate to your personal life and background.

TIP 7: Check your understanding.

As you read, stop occasionally to check your understanding. One way to do this is to summarize in your mind what you have read so far. If you are reading nonfiction, list the main points in your mind. If you are reading a fictional story, list the main characters, the main problem they face, and the most important events.

If you can't briefly summarize what you have read, you probably need to go back and reread some part of the passage.

 TIP 8: Connect what you see to what you have read.

If a passage contains pictures or diagrams, take time to look at them and see how they relate to the ideas in the passage. What important information do they add to the passage? Why do you think the author chose to include them?

7. How does the illustration help you to understand the passage?

_____

_____

_____

 TIP 9: When you finish reading, summarize the passage in your mind.

When you finish reading, go back and skim for the main points. Then summarize them in your mind. Also, ask yourself, *What is the main idea?* This will help you to check your understanding and to remember what you have learned.

8. Which of the following is the best summary of the selection?

A. The yo-yo was supposed to be a toy used by children, but it was soon made into a very helpful hunting tool.

B. The yo-yo was mostly used by the rich and famous during the French Revolution.

C. Yo-yos are difficult to use but, with a lot of practice, anybody can learn to do the best tricks.

D. Over the years, the yo-yo went from being a hunting tool to a popular toy that some yo-yoists call a sport.

9. Write a one- or two-sentence summary of each of the three sections in the passage.

A. From Tool to Toy

_____

_____

_____

B. The Yo-Yo in America

_____

_____

_____

C. A New Sport

_____

_____

_____

10. Which sentence from the passage best describes the main idea of the whole passage?

A. Loop the Loop is one of the most popular yo-yo tricks at competitions.

B. The yo-yo didn't get its official name until it came to America.

C. The yo-yo has changed from hunting tool to a popular toy and sport.

D. The yo-yo was used by ancient Egyptians and Greeks.

TIP 10: Talk to others about the passage.

Share your ideas and questions with a classmate or teacher who also has read the passage. You each may have ideas the other hasn't thought of.

 TIP 11: Record what you have learned.

If you are reading to learn or to gather information, you may want to record what you find. You can do this by writing a summary, creating an outline, or writing notes in a K-W-L chart. You may also want to list any questions the passage has raised in your mind. These notes will help you go beyond the passage to learn more about the topic.

11. What did you learn from "Know the Yo!" Record the information you learned in the right-hand column of the K-W-L chart on page 49.

Here are a few more questions about the passage.

12. Which experience would probably help you understand this passage best?

   A. watching a television program about Napoleon

   B. watching yo-yoists compete in a yo-yo championship

   C. learning how to tie knots in string

   D. researching hunting tools at the library

13. The information in this passage would be least helpful to someone writing a report on which of the following topics?

   A. Egyptian temples

   B. yo-yo tricks

   C. ancient toys

   D. interesting new sports

TIP 12: Use other strategies to understand what you read.

Here are a few more ways to understand the things you read:

- **Use the PQRR method.** *Preview* the reading. Ask *questions* before, during, and after the reading. *Reread* the difficult parts, and *record* what you learned.

- **Read difficult parts aloud.** Hearing a passage read aloud can help with understanding.

- **Use a journal or learning log to help you think through ideas.** Describe how the reading has helped you grow or changed the way you view the topic.

- **Express your ideas and feelings about the writing through a work of art.** Whether you enjoy drawing, painting, sculpting, writing poetry, or another art form, responding to writing through art can help you to understand how you feel about the writing.

- **Check other sources.** If you are still having trouble understanding a passage, or if you just want to find out more about a topic, try your local library. Resources such as encyclopedias, dictionaries, magazines, and so on can offer more information to sink your teeth into. People who are knowledgeable about the topic also can help. You'll learn more about resources in Lesson 12 of this book.

Reading Practice

Directions: Read the passage and answer the questions that follow.

Trading Places

by Sheena George

Trish and Carly are best friends, even though they come from different backgrounds. When Carly's family faces difficult times, the two girls find out how much they have in common.

Every day after school, Trish would go to Carly's house until Trish's mother finished work and picked her up. This had been going on for almost a year. Still, Trish remained in awe of certain things about Carly's home.

The carpet. Walking on it was like stepping onto a cloud. Of course, you took off your shoes at the door. Trish's apartment had hard, linoleum floors. There, nobody took off their shoes because their feet would freeze.

The soap. Carly's bathroom had a beach theme. In her bathroom, the soap was shaped like starfish. Who ever heard of soap coming in different shapes?

Her mother. Carly's mother was always home. She did not have to work. And Carly's mother talked to Carly, and even Trish, as if they were grown up. She never bossed them around. Every afternoon, Carly's mother would receive a phone call from Carly's father. "I love you, too," were always her last words. For a long time, Trish thought that Carly's dad lived far away. Then Carly explained that he liked to call before he came home from work.

On top of that, Carly had every type of video game, even some that Trish had never heard of. Trish had stopped asking for video games because she knew that her mother could not buy them.

One day Carly did not show up for school. It was strange because Trish had been at her house the day before. Halfway through the morning, she began to hear rumors. There had been a fire at Carly's house. Nobody was hurt. The Red Cross was handling things. Still, Trish was sad all day. In one corner of her mind, she pictured a starfish, melting.

At the very end of the day, a straggly-haired Carly appeared at Trish's locker holding a teddy bear.

"Hey there. Whatcha doing?" Carly asked.

"Worrying about you, that's what!" Trish cried. "What happened? How did you get here?"

"My folks just dropped me off. Hey, do you mind if I come over?"

"To my place?" Trish stammered.

"Yeah. It's been a rough day."

Trish had hesitated. And once she hesitated, she could not hide the fact that she had hesitated. Her best friend could have died in a fire, and here she was worried about a little mess. It wasn't just the mess, though. She said, "Well, there's really nothing to do there." She was also thinking about how all they had in the refrigerator was some cheese and a carton of milk.

It was as if Carly read her mind. "It doesn't matter. At least your place doesn't smell like smoke."

On the bus ride, Carly told Trish about the fire. No one had been home. They had come home to chaos. All of her stuff was ruined by the smoke and water. She was supposed to make a list of things she lost for the insurance company. "After a while, you just don't care," Carly said. "I mean, it's just stuff, right?" Strangely enough, Trish knew just how she felt.

The moment of truth arrived. Trish opened the door to the apartment, fearing what she might see. "Whatever you do, don't take off your shoes," she said. "You could get hurt."

Carly's laugh put her at ease. "It's okay. *Really*," she said with a smile.

"I guess there *is* a lot to do here. A lot of cleaning!" Trish said.

"I'm game," Carly said.

"That was a joke."

"No, really. I'd like to. I want to. It might take my mind off things."

Trish said, "I guess we could start with the dishes."

"Great! You'll teach me how?"

"Wha—?"

"We have a dishwasher, remember?"

As it turned out, there was a lot that Carly had never done before. She had never mopped a floor, either. But she caught on quickly. The two worked like a tornado, taking a break only for a cheese and cracker snack. In a couple of hours, they were seated on Trish's bed, playing cards.

"You should come over more often," Trish said. "We could trade places."

"Well, cleaning's not so bad, but I sure as heck don't want to do it every day," Carly said, grinning.

"I think I'd keep the house picked up if I knew I was going to have a friend over."

Carly looked at her and smiled.

"Is it a deal?" Trish asked, handing her the deck of cards.

"Deal," Carly said, as she shuffled the next hand.

1. What would be the best way to preview this passage?

    A. Read the first and last paragraphs of the selection.

    B. Look at the title, introduction, and illustration.

    C. Scan the selection for the words *Red Cross*.

    D. Skim the subheadings of the selection for the key ideas.

2. What type of passage is this?

    A. fiction

    B. nonfiction

    C. poetry

    D. drama

3. Which sentence summarizes the information in paragraphs 2 through 5?

   A. Trish is angry at her mother for working all the time.

   B. Carly doesn't really like Trish for who she is.

   C. Trish thinks that Carly's home life seems perfect.

   D. Trish's home life is beginning to affect her grades.

4. Complete the following graphic organizer:

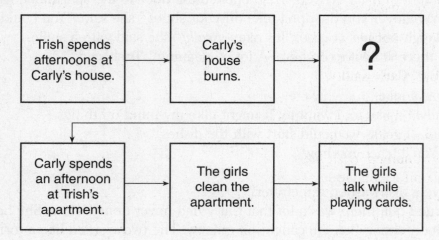

   A. Carly offers to help clean up again.

   B. Carly shares her story with Trish.

   C. Trish wonders where star-shaped soap comes from.

   D. Trish teaches Carly how to wash dishes.

5. Based on paragraph 2, what do you know about Trish's apartment?

   A. It's far away.

   B. It has new floors.

   C. It's messy.

   D. It's small.

6. What is the main idea of this story?

   A. A girl named Carly is upset because she has lost all her belongings in a house fire.

   B. Two girls who are best friends spend time at each other's homes each day after school.

   C. A girl named Trish feels uncomfortable about inviting friends to her house because her mom isn't home.

   D. Two girls from different backgrounds deepen their friendship after one loses her possessions in a fire.

7. What is the theme of this story?

   A. No one's life is perfect.

   B. Nothing in life is ever free.

   C. It's better to be safe than sorry.

   D. It is important to be prepared.

8. Why is Trish worried about Carly coming over to her house? Support your answer with details from the story.

_____

_____

_____

_____

_____

_____

_____

_____

Looking into Literature

Imagine you're walking through the forest on a sunny spring afternoon. You follow a narrow path into a clearing. In the middle of the clearing sits a small hut. You walk inside to find a glowing ball on a table in the center of the hut. When you look into the ball, you hear an echoey voice–

> "Welcome. Please state the kind of story you would like to experience. Keep your eyes in their forward-facing position, and wait a moment for your adventure to begin."

What kind of story would you want to experience? Would you visit a time and place in history, or check out things that haven't even happened yet? Maybe you would rather leave the earth altogether and enter a completely different world.

Reading is a little bit like having a crystal ball. Through literature, you can visit almost any time or place you want to go. But it isn't magic—all you have to do is open a book, read what's inside, and set your imagination free.

In this unit, you will learn about the tools an author uses to build a good story, poem, or play. If the author uses these tools well, you might feel as if you are right there in the story, watching it happen.

In This Unit

Story Elements

Poetry Elements

Drama Elements

The Author's Tools

Lesson 5: Story Elements

What is your favorite kind of story? Do you like solving a spooky mystery, or feeling the love in a romance novel? Do you like to turn out the lights and read a horror story under your bed covers with a flashlight? Maybe you like imaginary looks into the future with a science fiction story. Perhaps your favorite books make your heart pound as you read an exciting adventure.

No matter what kind you like best, most stories share some common elements. If you tried to write the shortest possible description of a story, it might look like this:

Something happens to *someone, somewhere.*

The "something" that happens is the **plot**, or the action of the story. The "someone" is the story's main **character(s)**. The "somewhere" is called the **setting**. In a good story, the plot, character, and setting all work together to create an experience for the reader.

In this lesson, you'll read two stories, each set during a different time in history. As you read, notice how each story is affected by the time and place in which it is set.

Read the following passage. It will be used to help you understand the tips in this lesson.

adapted from

Rip Van Winkle

by Washington Irving

Rip Van Winkle is a lazy man who is dissatisfied with his life. One day, while squirrel hunting in New York's Catskill Mountains, he decides to stop and take a nap. He awakens twenty years later to find that the world around him has changed.

As Rip neared the village, he met a number of people, none of whom he knew. This somewhat surprised him, for he thought he knew everyone in the country 'round. Their dress, too, was of a different fashion from that which he had grown used to. Those he met were equally surprised upon seeing him, and all stopped and stared and rubbed their chins. This repeated gesture caused Rip, involuntarily, to do the same. When he did so, to his amazement, he found that his beard had grown a foot long!

He now entered the outskirts of the village. A troop of strange children ran at his heels, hooting after him and pointing at his gray beard. The dogs, too, not one of which he recognized as an old friend, barked at him as he passed.

The very village was changed. It was larger, and with many more people. There were rows and rows of houses which he had never seen before, and those which had been familiar to him had disappeared. Strange names hung over the doors, strange faces peeked out from the windows—everything was strange. . .

He now hurried forth to his old haunt, the village inn, but it, too, was gone. A large, rickety wooden building stood in its place, with great gaping windows, some of them broken and mended with old hats and petticoats. Over the door was painted "The Union Hotel by Jonathan Doolittle." Instead of the great tree that once sheltered the quiet little Dutch inn in the past, there was now a tall pole with something on top that looked like a red nightcap, and from it fluttered a flag, on which was arranged a collection of stars and stripes.

All this Rip found impossible to understand. He recognized on the sign, however, the ruby face of King George, under which he had relaxed so many a peaceful evening. But, alas, even this had been changed. The red coat was exchanged for a blue one, and a sword was held in the hand instead of a scepter.[1] The head was decorated with a tilted hat, and underneath was painted in large letters, "General Washington."

There was, as usual, a crowd of old people about the door, but none that Rip recognized. The very character of the people seemed different. There was a busy, bustling, angry tone about it, instead of the usual lack of concern and drowsy peacefulness. He looked in vain for the wise Nicholas Vedder, with his broad face and double chin, or for Van Bummel, the schoolmaster, complaining about the contents of an old newspaper. In place of these, he saw a lean, grumpy-looking fellow, with his pockets full of handbills,[2] arguing

---

[1] **scepter:** a staff or baton that represents the authority of a royal person

[2] **handbills:** flyers or pamphlets

forcefully about the rights of citizens . . . elections . . . members of Congress . . . liberty . . . Bunker Hill . . . heroes of seventy-six . . . All these were perfect nonsense to the bewildered Van Winkle.

The appearance of Rip, with his long, grizzled beard, his rusty fowling piece,[3] his sloppy dress, and an army of women and children at his heels, soon attracted the attention of the tavern politicians. They crowded around him, eyeing him from head to foot with great curiosity. The speaker hurried up to him, drew him aside, and asked him "on which side he voted." Rip stared at him blankly. Another short but busy little fellow pulled him by the arm and, rising on tiptoe, whispered in his ear, "Are you Federal or Democrat?" Rip was equally at a loss to understand the question.

Then a knowing, self-important old gentleman, in a sharp tilted hat, made his way through the crowd. He planted himself before Rip Van Winkle, with one hand on his hip, the other resting on his cane, and his keen eyes penetrating into Rip's very soul. He asked in a serious tone what brought him to the election with a gun on his shoulder and a mob at his heels and whether he meant to start a riot in the village.

"Alas! Gentlemen," cried Rip in confusion, "I am a poor, quiet man, a native of this area, and a loyal subject of the king, God bless him!"

Here a general shout burst from the crowd: "A Tory![4] A Tory! A spy! A refugee! Hustle him! Away with him!"

> ### Behind the Writing
>
>
>
> **WASHINGTON IRVING
> (1783–1859)**
>
> Washington Irving is one of early America's most important writers. He helped make the short story a popular form of literature and was also one of the first American authors to earn widespread fame in Europe. Irving was born in New York City. He started writing when he was just a teenager and published his first work in a New York City newspaper in 1803. Two of Irving's best-known stories are "Rip Van Winkle" and "The Legend of Sleepy Hollow."

---

[3] **fowling piece:** a shotgun used for hunting birds or other small animals

[4] **Tory:** a person who supported the British king and was against independence for the colonies during the American Revolution

TIP 1: Identify who is telling the story.

A story's **narrator** is the person telling the story. Some narrators are characters within the story. They mention themselves by using personal pronouns such as *I, me, myself, we,* and *our.* They tell the story based on how they think and feel. These are called **first-person narrators**. Stories told in this way are said to be in first-person point of view.

A **first-person point of view** includes only the events that the narrator sees, is a part of, or knows about second-hand. Think of a first-person narrator as being right inside the story, a part of the action. Here is an example:

> Last night, my brother Andrew and I lay awake in our beds, listening to the storm. I was worried that a bolt of lightning would strike our half-built tree-house. Something more serious seemed to be on Andrew's mind, though. When the lightning flashed, I could see him clutching the bedspread beneath his chin. His face seemed filled with fear. I knew he wasn't scared of storms, so I couldn't help wondering, *What's up with him?*

A **third-person narrator** is not a character in the story. This type of narrator describes the characters and events in a story without being a part of the action. He or she acts more like an invisible observer who sees and hears everything that takes place. Third-person narrators do not mention themselves at all. Here is an example:

> Andrew and Peter lay awake in their beds, listening to the storm. Peter was mostly worried about lightning striking their half-built tree house. Andrew had other things to think about. He felt there was something creepy about this old house their family had just moved into. The night before, he was sure he heard strange clanking noises coming from the attic. Now this storm was bringing all his fears to life. It seemed like a perfect night for a haunting.

Now answer some point-of-view questions about "Rip Van Winkle."

1. Which point of view does the author use in "Rip Van Winkle"? Circle the correct answer.

   first-person   third-person

2. How do you know?

   _____

   _____

   _____

   _____

TIP 2: Determine the mood of the passage.

The author's voice sets the mood of the passage. A **mood** is a general feeling. An author tells a story using his or her own voice. An author's voice is a lot like your speaking voice. When you are excited, your voice sounds very different than it does when you are sad. Authors use their voices to show the mood of a story, too.

When you read, listen for the author's voice, and figure out what mood it is expressing. The mood in a story or scene might be scary, exciting, sad, relaxed, mysterious, humorous, suspenseful, and so on.

3. In "Rip Van Winkle," the mood in the tavern can best be described as

    A. creepy.

    B. cheerful.

    C. tense.

    D. calm.

4. Circle details in "Rip Van Winkle" that helped you answer Number 3.

 TIP 3: Identify details that describe the characters.

Character details can take many forms. Authors make their characters by including details about a character's looks, thoughts, feelings, actions, and speech. Everything about that character makes up who he or she is. Paying attention to these details will help you learn a lot about what a character is like.

One of the ways authors create great stories is by giving them interesting major characters. **Major characters** are the most important people in the story. They usually create most of the action. They are called "round" or "three-dimensional" because the author has described them so well that they seem like real people. **Minor characters**, on the other hand, are simple. They are sometimes called "flat" because we don't know very much about them. Minor characters are not as important to the story, so they may be described in only a few words and may show only a few emotions.

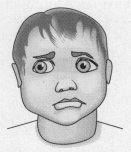

Three-dimensional Character

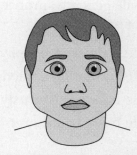

One-dimensional Character

Here are some questions to ask yourself about the main character:

- What is the character like?
- What does the character want most? Why?
- What is the main problem the character faces?
- How does the character view his or her situation?
- How does he or she get along with other characters in the story?
- How does the character change throughout the story?
- How does the character's personality affect what happens in the story?

5. Use the following character web to note details about Rip Van Winkle. List as many details as you can find in the passage. You may draw additional branches of the web if you like.

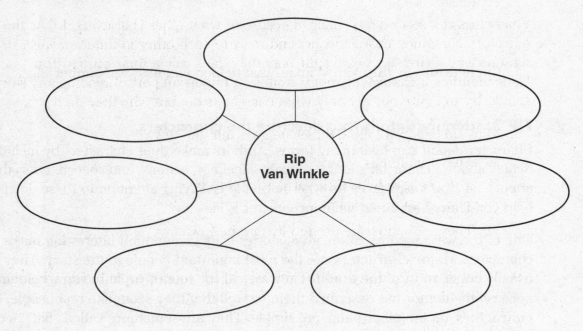

Use the details you gathered in Number 5 to answer the following questions.

6. The villagers are surprised by Rip's appearance for all of the following reasons except which one?

A. He is dressed sloppily.
B. He is wearing a tilted hat.
C. He is carrying a rusty fowling piece.
D. He has a beard over a foot long.

7. How does Rip feel about what he sees in the village?

   A. angry

   B. happy

   C. amused

   D. puzzled

 TIP 4: Notice how and why the relationships between the characters change.

The characters in most stories don't stay the same. Usually, the characters change the way they act or think by the end of the story. They may learn an important lesson, defeat an enemy, or find something they've been missing, to name just a few possibilities. They may also change their opinion or **viewpoint** about something.

Characters in a story often change because of what other characters do. As the action of a story continues, characters act and react to each other in different ways. The reasons why characters behave the way they do is called their **motivation**. Understanding a character's motivation is an important part of reading any story. You should try to figure out not only what characters do, but why they do it.

8. Why do children follow Rip as he goes into the town?

   A. They think he is a Tory.

   B. They believe he is General Washington.

   C. They think he looks funny.

   D. They remember he used to live in the town.

9. What word best describes the reaction of the townspeople to Rip when he first enters town?

   A. boredom

   B. fear

   C. anger

   D. curiosity

10. By the end of the passage, how do the townspeople's feelings toward Rip change?

    A. They think he is an enemy.

    B. They are curious to hear about his long sleep.

    C. They are happy he is home.

    D. They recognize him as a long-lost friend.

11. What causes this change in the townspeople's feelings about Rip?

_____

_____

_____

 TIP 5: Identify details that describe the setting.

Details that describe setting might include the point in history, the season, the time of day, the weather, the location, the landscape, and so on. All of these things can add to your understanding of a story.

12. Where and when does this scene from "Rip Van Winkle" take place?

_____

_____

13. Underline details in the story to support your answer to Number 12.

14. What important event has taken place during Rip's 20-year nap?

_____

_____

The Plot Is Where the Action Is

The **plot** is what happens in a story. Plots usually have a beginning, a middle, and an end. Most plots are structured something like the following diagram:

In the beginning of a story, the foundation for the story is laid: we find out who is in the story, where the story takes place, and what problem will shape the story. After the introduction, the story is set up like the way you set a table with china and silverware to get ready for dinner. The rising action is when all the pieces are put into place for the climax, which is like the dinner or party you've been preparing for. During the climax, the big events happen that determine how the problem(s) in the story will be resolved. After the climax, the clean-up begins: characters react to the climax and smaller events happen because of it. Finally, the table is cleared and all the pieces are put back into place—sometimes things go back to the way they were when the story started, and sometimes everything has changed.

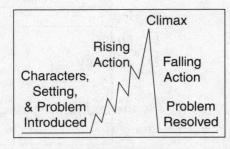

TIP 6: Find the conflict in a scene or story.

Most plots are based on conflict. The **conflict** is the main problem the character faces. Characters might have conflicts with other characters, with nature, or with themselves. If a character has a conflict with herself, she might be trying to study for a difficult math test or soccer game.

15. What is Rip Van Winkle's main problem?

    A. He is being followed by a crowd of women and children.

    B. He is faced with changes he does not understand.

    C. He is a Tory and a loyal supporter of the king.

    D. He is unshaven, his clothes are ragged, and his gun is rusty.

16. How is his problem affected by the setting of the story?

_____

_____

 TIP 7: Follow the plot to learn how the conflict is solved.

The story unfolds as the character or characters face the problem and try to solve it. You can use a graphic organizer to help you follow the plot. Look at the following story map.

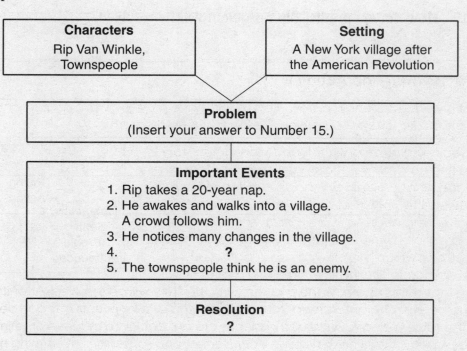

17. Which of the following best fits next to Number 4 under "Important Events"?

    A. He goes hunting in the mountains.

    B. He becomes dissatisfied with his life.

    C. He goes to an inn and is questioned.

    D. He notices that his beard has grown.

Paying attention to causes and effects also can help you follow the plot. A story may start with an event that causes several effects. Other stories might have a long chain of events that cause other events, building on each other. Look for these relationships between events in a story, where one event leads to another. These are sometimes signaled with words and phrases such as *therefore, as a result, because of, thus*, and so on. (You will learn more about cause-and-effect relationships in Lesson 9.)

18. What causes the townspeople to call Rip a spy?

    A. He says he is loyal to the king.

    B. He does not tell how he votes.

    C. He says he is a Democrat.

    D. He starts a riot in the village.

Eventually there will be a climax to the story. A **climax** is a main event in which the problem must be either solved or accepted once and for all. As the story ends and the conflict is resolved, we also may see how the character is changed because of his or her experiences.

19. How do you predict Rip's problem will be resolved?

_____

_____

_____

_____

TIP 8: The events of the plot connect the past, present, and future actions of characters.

Often, what a character does at certain points in a story relates to what he or she did earlier in the story, or what he or she will do later on in the story. For example, a character who loses a race at the beginning of a story may choose to practice running, and win his or her next race at the end of the story. In this way, actions at the beginning of the story affect actions later in the story.

Outside events can also influence a character. When Rip wakes up, he has no idea what has taken place while he was sleeping. He doesn't realize that the people of his village no longer serve King George. Because he is unaware of the events that have taken place in his village, he tells the crowd that he is a loyal subject of the king, which ends up getting him into trouble.

 TIP 9: Use what you learn about the characters, setting, and plot to determine the theme of the story.

You learned in Lesson 1 that a theme is the main message or lesson the author wants to share through the writing. One way to figure out the theme in a fictional story is to ask yourself what lessons the characters learn.

20. What is the theme of the scene you read from "Rip Van Winkle"?

   A. Times change, even if people don't.

   B. Absence makes the heart grow fonder.

   C. Treat others as you want to be treated.

   D. Time heals all wounds.

 TIP 10: Pay attention to the historical parts of the story.

The story you just read is not only about a man who wakes up from a really long nap. It is also about a time of great changes in American history. The author transports us to the past, using history to tell a story or telling a story about history. When the author gives hints in the story about real historical events, this information helps us understand why Rip is so confused.

21. Why are the townspeople upset when Rip says he is loyal to the king?

   A. Because the king is cruel and unjust to the townspeople.

   B. Because they believe he is lying about his loyalty to their king.

   C. Because they think he is the king himself.

   D. Because the king is no longer the leader of their land.

When you read a story set in a past historical period, ask yourself how the setting affects characters and events in the story.

TIP 11: Notice how the author's tone makes you feel about the subject.

In Tip 2, you learned that the mood of a story is the general "feeling" of the story. **Tone** is the way someone speaks. Tone can help set the story's mood. An author's tone can be positive, negative, or neutral. Neutral means neither positive or negative, but in the middle.

Sometimes a passage's tone can help you learn about the author's point of view. No matter what kind of writing authors do, they always have ideas and opinions about their topic.

Other times, authors want to get their feelings and opinions across to the reader. Whether it's fiction or nonfiction, this kind of writing usually has a more personal tone. It's easier to decide how the author feels about the subject or characters he or she is writing about.

Look back at "Rip Van Winkle" and answer the questions that follow. Keep in mind that the author, Washington Irving, was born just after the American Revolution and probably grew up learning about those events.

22. From the tone of the writing, how do you think the author feels about politics?

    A. He wishes more people would help make changes.

    B. He believes things basically stay the same over time.

    C. He thinks big changes can happen in a short time.

    D. He doesn't care about political events.

23. What makes you think the author feels that way?

_____

_____

_____

It's important to recognize how authors feel about the subjects they write about because their viewpoint affects what they write, and what they write can affect how you as the reader feel about the subject.

TIP 12: Judge how well the author did his or her job.

Stories can be just like real life. They also can be as unreal as a story filled with fairies, elves, and flying dragons. A story can take your imagination to all sorts of places.

When reading fiction, you are probably willing to enter the world the author creates. Never mind whether the events could happen in the real world—as long as they make sense in the world of the story.

For example, in "Rip Van Winkle," you know that Rip's 20-year nap couldn't really happen. Nobody could survive that long in the real world without food and water. You probably recognized that this part of the story is imaginary. You were also probably willing to go along with it—as long as the author could make it seem real.

But what if Rip had started talking in 21st-century slang? If Rip had said something like, "Yo! That was one long nap I took!" the story would no longer be as believable.

Whether the story could happen or could never happen, the plot, setting, and characters must be believable in order for the story to work. If the author does a good job, even the wildest plot, setting, and characters can make for an interesting story.

Here are a few questions to ask yourself when evaluating an author's work:

- Are the characters believable? Do they act in ways that seem to fit their personalities?

- Is it a story that could happen or an imaginary story that could never happen? If the story is meant to be realistic, is it believable, based on your own experiences of the real world? If the story is fantasy, does the author create a world that you are willing to believe in—if only during the time you spend reading the book?

- Is the plot believable? Do the events seem possible within the world the author creates?

Sometimes authors mix realism and fantasy in the stories they write. In "Rip Van Winkle," Rip's 20-year nap is fantasy, but the descriptions of an early American town—the people, places, and politics—are believable.

24. Does Rip Van Winkle act the way you would expect someone to act who has slept for 20 years through historic changes in society?

_____

_____

_____

_____

_____

_____

25. Underline details in the story to support your answer to Number 24.

26. What historical figures are mentioned in the story?

_____

_____

Reading Practice

Directions: Read the passage and answer the questions that follow.

from

Number the Stars

by Lois Lowry

Annemarie Johansen and Ellen Rosen are best friends who live in Denmark during World War II. Denmark has been taken over by Germany, and soldiers are stationed on every street corner in their city.

"I'll race you to the corner, Ellen!" Annemarie adjusted the thick leather pack on her back so that her schoolbooks balanced evenly. "Ready?" She looked at her best friend.

Ellen made a face. "No," she said, laughing. "You know I can't beat you—my legs aren't as long. Can't we just walk, like civilized people?" She was a stocky ten-year-old, unlike lanky Annemarie.

"We have to practice for the athletic meet on Friday—I *know* I'm going to win the girls' race this week. I was second last week, but I've been practicing every day. Come on, Ellen," Annemarie pleaded, eyeing the distance to the next corner of the Copenhagen[1] street. "Please?"

Ellen hesitated, then nodded and shifted her own rucksack of books against her shoulders. "Oh, all right. Ready," she said.

"Go!" shouted Annemarie, and the two girls were off, racing along the residential sidewalk. Annemarie's silvery blond hair flew behind her, and Ellen's dark pigtails bounced against her shoulders.

"Wait for me!" wailed little Kirsti, left behind, but the two older girls weren't listening.

Annemarie outdistanced her friend quickly, even though one of her shoes came untied as she sped along the street called Østerbrogade, past the small shops and cafés of her neighborhood here in northeast Copenhagen. Laughing, she skirted an elderly lady in black who carried a shopping bag made of string. A young woman pushing a baby in a carriage moved aside to make way. The corner was just ahead.

Annemarie looked up, panting, just as she reached the corner. Her laughter stopped. Her heart seemed to skip a beat.

"Halte!" the soldier ordered in a stern voice.

---

[1] **Copenhagen:** the capital of Denmark

The German word was as familiar as it was frightening. Annemarie had heard it often enough before, but it had never been directed at her until now.

Behind her, Ellen also slowed and stopped. Far back, little Kirsti was plodding along, her face in a pout because the girls hadn't waited for her.

Annemarie stared up. There were two of them. That meant two helmets, two sets of cold eyes glaring at her, and four tall shiny boots planted firmly on the sidewalk, blocking her path to home.

And it meant two rifles, gripped in the hands of the soldiers. She stared at the rifles first. Then, finally, she looked into the face of the soldier who had ordered her to halt.

"Why are you running?" the harsh voice asked. His Danish was very poor. Three years, Annemarie thought with contempt. Three years they've been in our country, and still they can't speak our language.

"I was racing with my friend," she answered politely. "We have races at school every Friday, and I want to do well, so I—" Her voice trailed away, the sentence unfinished. Don't talk so much, she told herself. Just answer them, that's all.

Behind the Writing

LOIS LOWRY
(1937–)

Lois Lowry was born in Honolulu, Hawaii. She won the 1990 Newbery Medal for *Number the Stars*, which tells the daring story of a girl who tries to help her best friend, a Jewish girl, escape from the Nazis. Lowry also won the 1994 Newbery Medal for *The Giver*. Lowry measures her success as a writer by her ability to "help adolescents answer their own questions about life, identity, and human relationships."

1. How does the setting most affect the plot in this scene from *Number the Stars*?

   A. The scene takes place in Denmark, where people mainly speak Danish.

   B. The scene takes place on an afternoon, when many people are out and about.

   C. The scene takes place during a war, when threatening soldiers are everywhere.

   D. The scene takes place on a busy sidewalk, where too many people are walking.

2. Read these sentences from the passage.

   "You know I can't beat you—my legs aren't as long. Can't we just walk, like civilized people?" She was a stocky ten-year-old, unlike lanky Annemarie.

   What does *lanky* mean?

   A. tall and thin

   B. short and thin

   C. tall and stocky

   D. short and stocky

3. Who is telling this story?

    A. a first-person narrator named Ellen

    B. a first-person narrator named Annemarie

    C. a third-person narrator named Kirsti

    D. a third-person narrator not in the story

4. Which experience would most help a reader to understand this story?

    A. participating in a school athletic competition

    B. talking to someone who lived in Denmark during World War II

    C. visiting a museum with an exhibit on the history of the American military

    D. having an annoying little sister

5. Which of the following best describes the character of Annemarie?

    A. shy

    B. cruel

    C. brave

    D. thoughtless

6. Which statement best completes the graphic organizer?

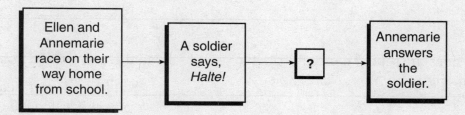

    A. Annemarie outdistances Ellen.

    B. The girls enter a race at school.

    C. The soldier asks why they are running.

    D. Kirsti is left behind as the two girls race.

7. How does the author show that the soldiers frighten Annemarie?

    A. by describing their appearance through Annemarie's eyes

    B. by having Annemarie say that she is afraid

    C. by showing the soldiers arresting Annemarie

    D. by showing Annemarie trembling and beginning to cry

8. Is this story an example of science fiction, historical fiction, folktale, or romance? How do you know? Use details from the story to support your answer.

_____

_____

_____

_____

_____

_____

_____

_____

Lesson 6: Poetry Elements

Have you sung any good poetry lately?

This might seem like a silly question, but whenever you sing along to country, rap, pop, or rock, you're singing a poem. Even if it doesn't rhyme or sound like a poem, song lyrics are a form of poetry. *Lyric*, in fact, is from the Greek word for "musical instrument." So when you read a poem, listen to the music it makes. A poem's words are carefully chosen and put together to create sounds and images that express ideas.

A poem is like a delicious dessert or a tart lemon: It is meant to be experienced, felt, and tasted. A poem is also intended to tell the reader something about the speaker's thoughts.

You don't need to know all the rules and rhyme patterns of poetry in order to read and enjoy it. You won't need to know those things for most reading tests. More than likely, the questions you'll see will be about the ideas and images in the poem. The following tips will help you understand—and enjoy—poetry. Here's a poem that uses sensory words. **Sensory words** are words that describe something we can taste, smell, hear, touch, or see.

Read the following poem. It will be used to help you understand some of the tips in this lesson.

from

Goblin Market

by Christina Rossetti

Morning and evening
Maids heard the goblins cry:
'Come buy our orchard fruits,
Come buy, come buy:
Apples and quinces,
Lemons and oranges,
Plump unpecked cherries,
Melons and raspberries,
Bloom-down-cheeked peaches,
Swart-headed mulberries,
Wild free-born cranberries,
Crab-apples, dewberries,
Pine-apples, blackberries,
Apricots, strawberries,
All ripe together
In summer weather,

(Continued on the following page)

Morns[1] that pass by,
Fair eves[2] that fly;
Come buy, come buy:
Our grapes fresh from the vine,
Pomegranates full and fine,
Dates and sharp bullaces,
Rare pears and greengages,
Damsons and bilberries,
Taste them and try:
Currants and gooseberries,
Bright-fire-like barberries,
Figs to fill your mouth,
Citrons from the South,
Sweet to tongue and sound to eye;
Come buy, come buy.'

"Buy from us with a golden curl"

[1] **morn:** short for morning

[2] **eves:** short for evenings

TIP 1: Get to know the different types of poetry.

People have been writing poems ever since there was language to write with. Since it is such an ancient art form, it has changed a lot over time. Different types of poems have been popular during different periods in history, and in different places around the world. Following are a few common types of poetry:

- **light verse** – funny or playful poetry, such as limericks

- **narrative poetry** – poetry that tells a story

- **haiku** – a form of Japanese poetry, usually made of only three lines

- **lyric poetry** – poetry with rhythms and sounds that give it a musical quality; often deals with personal topics

- **sonnet** – a poem with 14 lines, usually with an elaborate rhyme scheme

- **blank verse** – poetry with unrhymed lines but with a set syllable pattern or beat

- **free verse** – poetry that is free from fixed patterns of rhyme or beat

- **pattern poetry** – poems written so that the words form a certain pattern on the page

1. What type of poetry is "Goblin Market"?

   A. pattern poetry

   B. haiku

   C. narrative

   D. sonnet

TIP 2: Get to know the tools poets use.

Writers share a toolbox filled with things they can use to make their writing come alive. You probably already know about some of these tools. Others have special names you might not have heard. Learning about these tools can help you appreciate poetry, and understand what people mean when they discuss it. Here are a few terms that are often used to talk about poetry:

- Poems are usually made up of lines and stanzas. **Lines** are rows of words and **stanzas** are lines grouped together like paragraphs. *Stanza*, by the way, is an Italian word for *room*. You might think of each stanza of a poem as a room and ask yourself, *What kind of room is this?*

- **Rhythm** is the "beat" in a poem. Rap music uses rhythm heavily. If you read "Goblin Market" out loud, you can hear that it has a rhythm, too.

- An **image** is a word picture the poem paints in the reader's mind. Many of the descriptions of the different kinds of fruits in "Goblin Market" are images. Could you see what the poet was describing in your mind?

- **Repetition** is the use of the same sound, word, phrase, or line over and over. Songwriters often use this technique in song lyrics. In "Goblin Market," the poet repeats the line "Come buy, come buy" many times.

- An **analogy** is a comparison of two things. Simile and metaphor are two types of analogy. In "Goblin Market," the poet describes "bright-fire-like barberries," comparing the color of the berries to the color of fire. You will learn more about similes and metaphors later in this lesson.

- **Multiple-meaning words** are just what they sound like: words that can have more than one meaning. Poets often use multiple-meaning words to give hints about the deeper meaning of a poem.

- A **symbol** is something that stands for something else. For example, an eagle is commonly used as a symbol for freedom. The fruits in "Goblin Market" could be symbols of desire, or pleasure.

- **Dialect** is the spoken language of a person or group of people. It may be different from commonly accepted written language. Authors often use dialect to get the reader's attention or to help make their characters real. There are many different dialects in English. One example is slang.

- Poets sometimes use **invented words** to describe a feeling or an idea that there simply isn't a word for yet. Did you read books by Dr. Seuss when you were younger? (Or maybe just last week?) He invented hundreds of words in his poems.

- **Alliteration** is the repetition of two or more words that start with the same sound. "Percy pickled a peck of purple peas" is an example of alliteration.

- **Onomatopoeia** is the use of a word that sounds like what it is describing. The word *whoosh* is an example of this technique.

Some of these tools are specific to poetry (stanzas, for example, are only found in poems), but many can be found in fiction, nonfiction, and drama as well as in poetry.

 TIP 3: The first time you read through a poem, read for the main idea.

Poems may look different than other kinds of writing, but most are fairly easy to read. Some poems are like very short stories. Others are like jokes or riddles. Some are like pictures or snapshots created with words.

Don't get hung up on details the first time you read a poem. If a line seems difficult or confusing, just keep reading. Read for the main idea, the same as you would when reading a story. Try this tip as you read the poem.

Fast Food Chain

by John Hansen

There should be a diner
that's open all night
where busy wild beasts
could stop in for a bite.

The menu wouldn't have to be
very expensive
but to draw a good crowd
it should be fairly extensive.

There'd be caribou nuggets
for hungry wolf packs
and a thick grassy stew
for big hairy yaks.

There'd be fresh flopping fish
for slick barking seals
and quarter-ton plankton burgers
for enormous blue whales.

There'd be wild berry pizza
for grumbling grizzly bears
and dusty hay salads
for wild stallions and mares.

There'd be smelly dead stuff galore
for the jackals and buzzards
and cartons of french-fried flies
for fat toads and thin lizards.

There'd be rodents with cheese
for striped wild cats
and deluxe mosquito burritos
for squinty-eyed bats.

Wild animals' weird tastes
make up the food chain.
They all eat what they like,
no need to explain.

Which leads to a problem
that could be a bother:
What if the customers
start eating each other?

As you read the poem, did you get a feel for the overall idea of it? Was it serious or funny? Was it mostly about people or animals? Answer the following question based on the poem.

2. Which statement best describes the poem?

   A. a description of a person who opens a restaurant

   B. an explanation of how hard it is to feed animals

   C. a humorous look at what animals like to eat

   D. a scientific study of the food chain in nature

Now try it again, with another poem.

Lengths of Time
by Phyllis McGinley

Time is peculiar
And hardly exact.
Though minutes are minutes,
You'll find for a fact
(As the older you get
And the bigger you grow)
That time can
Hurrylikethis
Or plod, plod, slow.

Waiting for your dinner when you're hungry?
Down with the sniffles in your bed?
Notice how an hour crawls along and crawls along
Like a snail with his house upon his head.

But when you are starting
A game in the park,
It's morning,
It's noon,
And suddenly it's dark.
And hours like seconds
Rush blurringly by.
Whoosh!
Like a plane in the sky.

As you read the poem, did you get a feel for the overall idea of it? Are the sounds and images serious or lighthearted? Try the following question.

3. What is the poem mostly about?

    A. how hard it is to wait for dinner

    B. how we experience time

    C. games that last all day

    D. time moves faster as we grow older

TIP 4: Look for comparisons in the poem.

Poets are inventors. They use their imaginations to discover new ways of thinking about the world. One way they do this is by comparing things that usually aren't compared or by connecting things that are very different.

Writers often make comparisons using **figurative language**, words that describe things and ideas in a new and inventive way. The basic types of figurative language are described here.

A **simile** is a sentence that uses *like* or *as* to compare two things. "Venus Williams moves like lightning on the tennis court" is an example of simile.

4. Go back and reread the second stanza of "Lengths of Time." Underline one example of a simile in this stanza.

5. In "Lengths of Time," to what does the poet compare an hour in lines 12 and 13?

    A. a snail

    B. a house

    C. a minute

    D. a second

A **metaphor** is a sentence that makes a comparison without using *like* or *as*. It tells us that one thing *is* another. For example, a poet might say, "the moon is a giant pearl" or "the heat is a heavy blanket."

A metaphor is a more direct comparison than a simile, and it carries a stronger punch. "Mia is lightning" is a more powerful statement than "Mia moves like lightning."

6. In "Lengths of Time," what is the word *house* in line 13 actually describing?

    A. the poet's house

    B. a dead snail

    C. a snail's shell

    D. the snail's head

Hyperbole is making something bigger than it really is. When someone says, "I'll die if I can't go to that concert!" he or she is using hyperbole to show how strongly he or she feels.

Likewise, the goal of the writer may be to make a strong point about something or to get a laugh. In the last stanza of "Lengths of Time," the poet uses hyperbole to describe how fast time seems to go when you're doing something interesting: ". . . hours like seconds / Rush blurringly by."

Poets are using **personification** when they give animals or objects human qualities. Read the following poem.

The Poet Pencil

by Jesús Carlos Soto Morfín
translated by Judith Infante

Once upon a time a pencil wanted to write
poetry but it didn't have a point. One day a boy
put it into the sharpener, and in place of a point,
a river appeared.

7. What human characteristic does the poet give the pencil in this poem?

_____

_____

In this poem, the word *point* has both a concrete meaning and an abstract meaning. A **concrete** meaning describes something that is part of the physical world. An **abstract** meaning describes ideas that do not have physical detail. A point can be the tip of a sharp object, or it can be an idea that a writer wants to get across.

Word choice is one of the poet's most important tools. As in all kinds of writing, the specific details bring the ideas in the story or the poem to life. Poets like to use words that have multiple meanings to make a poem more interesting.

 TIP 5: Notice what the poem looks like.

Like the images and sounds in poems, poets also use sentence structure, line length, and punctuation to create meanings and moods. A long, one-sentence poem sounds smoother and seems to move faster than a poem with short sentences that force the reader to pause often. A poem that uses very little punctuation is going to feel more open and carefree than a poem, such as "Lengths of Time," with punctuation that creates a more exciting, nervous mood.

Line length also affects the mood and meaning of poems. Notice how the lines in the second stanza of "Lengths of Time" stretch out farther than the lines in the rest of the poem.

8. What is the second stanza of "Lengths of Time" mostly about?

    _____

As you can see, longer lines usually indicate slowness or a more relaxed mood. Here are a few more questions about "Lengths of Time."

9. Why are the words *hurrylikethis* run together in the poem?

    A. to confuse the reader

    B. to show that the older you get, the less you know

    C. to show that poets don't know how to spell

    D. time sometimes seems to move more quickly

10. What is the author's attitude toward time?

    A. angry

    B. sad

    C. fascinated

    D. disapproving

 TIP 6: Rhyme and rhythm are the music of poetry.

Read the following stanza.

from

Player Piano

by John Updike

My stick fingers click with a snicker   _____

And, chuckling, they knuckle the keys;   _____

Light-footed, my steel feelers flicker   _____

And pluck from these keys melodies.   _____

Not all poems rhyme, but many do. Reread the last stanza, and this time pay attention to which lines rhyme. If one line ends with "red" and another line ends with "bed," then you label both lines with the letter *a.* Then go through the poem and do the same thing with other lines that rhyme. This pattern is the poem's **rhyme scheme.**

11. Mark each pair of rhyming lines by lettering the pairs as *a* or *b* on the lines on page 91.

As you learned in Tip 2, rhythm is the "beat" of the poem, the way the words move. Try tapping your foot to "Player Piano" to feel its rhythm.

12. What mood or feeling do the rhythm and rhyme create in this poem?

_____

_____

 TIP 7: Read the poem again and again.

Do you like hearing your favorite song over and over? You can enjoy poetry in the same way. In fact, with many poems, the more you read them, the more you will understand and enjoy them.

Use the poems in this lesson to answer the following questions.

13. Which line of the poem "Goblin Market" contains an example of alliteration?

    A. Morning and evening

    B. All ripe together

    C. Dates and sharp bullaces

    D. Figs to fill your mouth

14. In the poem "Fast Food Chain," what does the poet mean by the lines, "They all eat what they like / no need to explain"?

    A. Animals are the owners of the restaurant.

    B. Animals don't know how to talk.

    C. Nature determines what animals like to eat.

    D. No one can describe an animal's eating behavior.

15. In the poem "Lengths of Time," which of the following words is an example of onomatopoeia?

    A. minutes

    B. hurry

    C. whoosh

    D. sky

16. Which of the following books would most likely contain poems like the one in the sidebar?

    A. *Collected Light Verse*

    B. *Narrative Poems for Adventurers*

    C. *Sonnets from Around the World*

    D. *The Four Seasons—A Book of Haiku*

Limericks

A **limerick** is a five-line poem with a rhyme scheme of *aabba*. Limericks are meant to be funny, with the last line delivering the "punch line."

My dearest old auntie named Anna	*a*
Makes her home in a giant banana.	*a*
Every night she must seal it	*b*
So the monkeys don't peel it	*b*
And devour her home sweet cabana!	*a*

—John Ham

Reading Practice

Directions: Read the passage and answer the questions that follow.

Old Dog Dreaming

by Greta Anderson

It starts with a few grunts and twitches.
The dream, like a locomotive
Setting off for distant lands,
Gains speed. Soon his paws are frantic,
    Devouring the ground between him and
What?—a deer, a hare, an antelope?
While his legs lay still with sleep.
Oh, how his chest heaves with the effort,
With every rise and fall a funny snort
    Or squeal, as if he were both pursuer
And the beast who is pursued.
How does the dream end?
Does he relive those glorious days
Before age settled into his joints
    And his gimpy gait and goofy smile
Made him the neighborhood mascot?
Before progress, like a locomotive,
Changed this land to lawns?
He would often catch what he chased,
    In this forested valley—
catch it and kill it and bring it home
Like his ancestor, the wolf.
If it is like human dreams, it ends
Just before the fatal act. It ends
    Midair, as the beast being chased
Meets the beast who chases it.
Perhaps he really is both.
Perhaps this dream is his way of wondering
What he might lose and what gain
    Could he return to the wilderness,
Of his young doghood,
What it might be like to have
Youth again, hot on his heels.

1. This poem is mostly about which of the following?

   A. an old dog dreaming of his youth

   B. an old dog dreaming that he is human

   C. an old dog dreaming that the city will one day become wilderness

   D. an old dog dreaming of what he will do when he wakes up

2. Read lines 2–4 from the poem:

   The dream, like a locomotive
   Setting off for distant lands,
   Gains speed . . .

   These lines contain which type of figurative language?

   A. simile

   B. metaphor

   C. personification

   D. hyperbole

3. The line "And his gimpy gait and goofy smile" is an example of which technique?

   A. rhyme

   B. metaphor

   C. hyperbole

   D. alliteration

4. What do the lawns in the fourth stanza symbolize?

   A. growing older

   B. oncoming trains

   C. the loss of the wilderness

   D. the extinction of the wolf

5. In the third stanza, the wilderness becomes a metaphor for

   A. the neighborhood.

   B. a train.

   C. progress.

   D. youth.

6. In what way does the poem personify the dog?

   A. by showing him moving as he sleeps

   B. by telling how he has aged over his lifetime

   C. by saying that he dreams as humans do

   D. by saying that he is well-known in his neighborhood

7. Which of the following is the main theme of the poem?

   A. Change comes to everything.

   B. People should follow their dreams.

   C. All wilderness should give way to progress.

   D. Pets should be tame and well-trained.

8. What do you think the dog in this poem was like when he was younger? Use details from the poem to support your answer.

_____

_____

_____

_____

_____

_____

_____

_____

Standards and Skills: 3.1, 3.5, 4.6

Lesson 7: Drama Elements

How does a story become a movie, television show, or play? A story uses paragraphs, dialogue, and descriptions to tell the tale. You picture the story in your mind as you read.

Think about what's different when you see a stage play, a TV program, or a movie. You don't have to picture the story in your mind—you can see it in front of you. What used to be in paragraphs, dialogue, and descriptions is now in the words and movements of the actors and in the people and places you see. The story has been dramatized by a **playwright**, an author who writes plays.

Drama is an ancient art form. People were writing plays long before they were writing novels. The first plays were written in Greece more than 2,600 years ago. These plays had no characters or dialogue, though. They were simply a group of actors speaking or singing together about the topic of the play. This group was called a

This art from ancient Greece shows a chorus of actors.

chorus, like groups of people who sing together today. A **chorus** is a group of actors speaking or singing together.

Then, a Greek playwright named Thespis changed everything. He put a single actor on stage with the chorus. This actor could speak back and forth with the leader of the chorus. This actor could also give a speech all by himself, called a **monologue**. Adding this actor to the play made the stories more interesting to the audience. Thespis is still known as the "Father of Drama." In fact, the word *thespian*, which means "actor," comes from the name Thespis.

Later, another Greek playwright, Aeschylus, brought in a second actor to work with the first. He also introduced the idea of using costumes and scenery to make the play more realistic. Pretty soon, Greek playwrights like Sophocles and Euripides were writing plays with three or more characters.

After the Greeks invented drama, the Romans and Europeans used it to express ideas about religion, and to retell old stories. William Shakespeare learned about the Greek and Roman playwrights as a boy in 16th century England. Many of the themes and ideas in his plays are similar to the themes and ideas in ancient Greek plays. Even today, people are still thinking about and retelling those ancient Greek stories.

In drama, the actors follow a **script** that tells them what to say. In this lesson, you will practice reading parts of a play's script. Read the following scenes from a tragedy by William Shakespeare. A **tragedy** is a play about misfortune and sad events. The scenes will be used to help you understand some of the tips in this lesson.

adapted from

The Tragedy of Hamlet, Prince of Denmark

by William Shakespeare

Shakespeare's famous tragedy Hamlet is considered by many to be the greatest play ever written. Its hero finds his world turned upside down by the death of his father. In these scenes, Hamlet receives news that will eventually destroy the lives of everyone around him.

CAST

HAMLET, prince of Denmark

HORATIO, his best friend, recently returned from abroad

MARCELLUS, a castle guard

GHOST, Hamlet's dead father

ACT I, SCENE IV

(At night outside the castle)

HAMLET: The air bites cleverly; it is very cold.

HORATIO: It is a nipping and a cutting air.

HAMLET: What hour is it now?

HORATIO: Just short of twelve.

MARCELLUS: No, I think it's struck.

HORATIO: Indeed? I did not hear. If so, it draws near the time when the spirit has been known to walk.

(A trumpet blasts from inside the castle.)

What's that?

HAMLET: It's just the King, my stepfather, swaggering[1] around as usual with his boot-licking[2] friends.

HORATIO: Is this the rule?

[1] **swaggering:** to walk around with more pride than one deserves

[2] **boot-licking:** following around a powerful person in order to receive favors

HAMLET: Yes, and I am now the exception.[3] Our court is now known for such empty celebrations. It's a blot on our reputation, just as certain heroes' honor is stained by some grave flaw.

(Enter GHOST.)

HORATIO: Look, my lord, it comes.

HAMLET: Angels and ministers of grace defend us! Whether you are a good spirit or an evil goblin, coming with purposes wicked or charitable, your form is such that I must call you Hamlet, King . . . father. Answer me! Tell me why your bones, blessed and buried, have returned, why the casket has cast you out. What does this mean, that your dead body walks again beneath the pale moon?

(GHOST calls HAMLET.)

HORATIO: It calls you to go away with it, as if it needed to speak to you alone.

MARCELLUS: Look how politely it seems to wave to you to come along. Whatever you do, don't go!

HORATIO: Don't go!

HAMLET: If it won't speak, I must follow.

HORATIO: Please don't!

HAMLET: Why, what do I have to lose? I do not care for my life here on earth. If it waves, I'll follow.

HORATIO: What if it lures you into the lake, or over some cliff, and then takes some other, far more terrible form? Think of it.

HAMLET: It waves. Go on, I'll follow.

MARCELLUS: You shall not go!

HAMLET: Let go of me!

HORATIO: Please, friend, do not persist.

[3] **exception:** to be left out alone

HAMLET: My fate cries out, steeling my nerves. Unhand me, gentlemen. I'll make a ghost of him that won't! I say, go away. Go on, I'll follow. *(Exit GHOST and HAMLET.)*

HORATIO: He's desperate.

MARCELLUS: Let's follow. It would be wrong to obey him now.

HORATIO: What will come of it all?

MARCELLUS: Something is rotten in the state of Denmark. *(Exit)*

SCENE V

(Enter GHOST and HAMLET.)

HAMLET: Where will you lead me? Speak, I'll go no further.

GHOST: Mark my words!

HAMLET: I will!

GHOST: The hour is almost come when I must throw myself into the flames.

HAMLET: Poor ghost!

GHOST: Don't pity me, but listen close to what I shall unfold.

HAMLET: Speak, I will listen.

GHOST: And so shall you look for revenge, when you hear.

HAMLET: What?

GHOST: I am your father's spirit, doomed to walk the night until my sins are cleansed by pain. Ah, I am not allowed to tell the secrets of my prison house, but if I could, they would freeze your blood and make every hair on your head stand on end. Instead, just listen. If you ever did love your father—

HAMLET: O, please!

GHOST: Revenge his foul and most unnatural murder.

HAMLET: Murder!

GHOST: Murder most foul, as it always is, but in this case, foul, strange, and unnatural.

HAMLET: Hurry your tale, so that I with wings as swift as thought may go to my revenge.

GHOST: I find you able enough. Now, Hamlet, hear: It is told that, while sleeping in my orchard, a serpent stung me. All the ears of Denmark are now ringing with this lie. The serpent that stung your father's life now wears his crown.

HAMLET: O my soul. My uncle?

GHOST: Yes, that beast, with his wicked skills did steal my wife, the queen. Her love turned from me and our marriage vows to that lowly serpent, as if feeding on garbage. But I must be brief. Morning draws near. As I was sleeping in my orchard, your uncle sneaked up with a bottle of poison, and poured the liquid into my ears. Like quicksilver,[4] it coursed through the gates and alleys of my body, and curdled[5] my blood, and stopped my heart. O horrible, O horrible most horrible! If you are a man, do not let this pass, but I command you, perform no ill deed against your mother. Let her soul work out its own curses. Now, I must away. The dawn's light is upon us. Whatever you do, remember me! *(Exit.)*

HAMLET: Remember you? What else can I do? Remember you? From my memory I'll wipe out everything else, all that I so patiently copied in school. That villain! O, here is the first note I shall take down (*gets out his tablet and, kneeling, begins to write*). That one may smile, and smile, and be a villain. *(Stands)* So, it seems, it may be in Denmark.

---

[4] **quicksilver:** mercury—a slick metallic liquid that can move on its own

[5] **curdled:** turned to cheese

TIP 1: Learn the terms used to talk about drama.

Being familiar with basic drama terms will help you enjoy drama more and understand it better. Some of these terms are used only for drama. Some of them are common to many other kinds of writing.

- **Acts** and **scenes** – how a play is divided. Each change of setting is a new scene. There can be more than one scene in an act and more than one act in a play. Think of acts as large chapters in a play, and scenes as smaller chapters within larger chapters.

- **Dialogue** – the words the characters say. In fiction, dialogue is placed in quotation marks. In drama, the dialogue is given without quotation marks, following the name of the character who speaks the line.

- **Narrator** – the "voice," or teller, of the story. In fiction, the narrator uses phrases such as "he said" and "she said," along with descriptions of the action. Many plays do not have narrators; the details of the action must be shown by the characters. If a play has a narrator, he or she usually gives less information than a narrator of a fictional story would. In some plays and movies, the narrator is never seen. This kind of narrator is called a **voice-over**.

- **Playwright** – the person who writes a script for a play. If the script is for a movie or television program, the writer is called a **screenwriter**.

- **Setting** – the time and place of the action. In a play, the setting is usually stated at the beginning of every scene.

- **Stage** – area within a theater upon which actors perform a play.

- **Stage directions** – words, often in brackets and italics, that tell the actor how to say the lines and how to move about on the stage. Stage directions usually are given in present tense.

- **Theater** – a building in which a play is performed.

Keep the scene from *The Tragedy of Hamlet, Prince of Denmark* in mind as you answer the following questions.

1. What is the main idea of this passage?

   A. Hamlet's friends try to stop him from following a ghost.

   B. Hamlet's uncle is ruining Denmark's reputation with parties.

   C. The ghost of Hamlet's father reveals that he was murdered by his brother.

   D. Hamlet promises to remember his father and writes about his uncle.

2. Fiction is divided into chapters; drama is divided into _____

   and _____.

3. The person who writes a play is called a _____. The written

   text is called a _____.

4. How does the setting affect the mood of the passage?

   _____

   _____

   _____

   _____

   _____

5. You and your friends want to put on a production of *Grease*, a musical. What
   would be the best way to decide how many actors you need for the show?

   A. Read the entire first act.
   B. Read the entire script.
   C. Read the cast of characters.
   D. Rent a DVD of the play.

6. The author gives information about Hamlet's father's murder through

   A. dialogue.
   B. stage directions.
   C. a narrator.
   D. a voice-over.

TIP 2: Learn to read "between the lines."

Each character's speeches are his or her **lines**. Between the lines are the stage directions. **Stage directions** tell *how* a character's lines should be spoken and how the actors should move about. When you are reading a play, the stage directions can help you picture the action in your mind.

7. Describe Hamlet's character, based on how he says his lines.

_____

_____

_____

_____

_____

8. Based on the section from the play, Hamlet's attitude about speaking with a ghost can best be described as

   A. brave.

   B. uncaring.

   C. afraid.

   D. excited.

TIP 3: **Understand the difference between narration and stage directions.**

Narrators may give a little or a lot of information about the characters and events in the story. Sometimes a play will have its own narrator who actually speaks to the audience.

Stage directions tend to be much shorter. Their main purpose is to tell the actors how to deliver their lines. Stage directions also tend to be given in present tense: as if they're happening now.

9. Try turning the following lines from the script into a story with a narrator.

   (GHOST calls HAMLET.)

   HORATIO: It calls you to go away with it, as if it needed to speak to you alone.

   MARCELLUS: Look how politely it seems to wave to you to come along. Whatever you do, don't go!

   HORATIO: Don't go!

   HAMLET: If it won't speak, I must follow.

   HORATIO: Please don't!

   HAMLET: Why, what do I have to lose? I do not care for my life here on earth. If it waves, I'll follow.

   HORATIO: What if it lures you into the lake, or over some cliff, and then takes some other, far more terrible form? Think of it.

   HAMLET: It waves. Go on, I'll follow.

   MARCELLUS: You shall not go!

   HAMLET: Let go of me!

   HORATIO: Please, friend, do not persist.

   HAMLET: My fate cries out, steeling my nerves. Unhand me, gentlemen. I'll make a ghost of him that won't! I say, go away. Go on, I'll follow. *(Exit GHOST and HAMLET.)*

   HORATIO: He's desperate.

Now, write your story on the lines below.

_____

_____

_____

_____

_____

_____

_____

_____

_____

_____

_____

_____

_____

_____

_____

 TIP 4: Imagine the script being performed on stage.

When a scene is acted out on stage, the setting becomes the **set**—whatever needs to be painted or built in order to make the setting clear. In *The Tragedy of Hamlet, Prince of Denmark*, the set might be in or near a castle. Objects that actors use in the scene are called stage properties, or **props**. A prop for Hamlet to carry might be a sword or a crown.

10. What prop would you need for Scene V in *The Tragedy of Hamlet, Prince of Denmark*?

    A. a trumpet

    B. a writing tablet

    C. a skull

    D. a bottle

Reading Practice

Directions: Read the passage and answer the questions that follow.

a one-act play based on

An Encounter with an Interviewer

by Mark Twain
adapted for the stage by Mike Acton

CAST OF CHARACTERS

MARK TWAIN, famous author and humorist
A young newspaper REPORTER

SETTING: 1870s. Curtains open to a darkened stage. Lights raise slowly showing a hotel room in a small town along the Midwestern route of Mr. Twain's speaking tour. The room is furnished in Victorian style with heavy drapery and highly decorated furniture, including a large, four-poster bed. MARK TWAIN, wearing his usual white linen suit, is seated in a high-back chair on one side of a small, round table. Across from him, the newspaper REPORTER, seated in an equally high and velvet-covered chair, seems anxious to begin the questioning. TWAIN appears friendly and eager, as if he were being interviewed for the first time from the front porch of his boyhood home in Hannibal, Missouri.

REPORTER: *(Leaning toward TWAIN)* Sir, if I could just ask you a few questions designed to bring out important points about your public and private life.

TWAIN: Oh, with pleasure, with pleasure. But I have a very bad memory. Sometimes I go weeks without remembering anything. Then, other weeks, I can remember dozens of things.

REPORTER: Will you do the best you can?

TWAIN: I will. I will put my whole mind to it.

REPORTER: Are you ready to begin?

TWAIN: Ready.

REPORTER: *(Opening his notebook and poising his pen)* How old are you?

TWAIN: *(Thinking for a moment)* Nineteen *(Pause)* in June.

REPORTER: Why, I would have taken you to be a much older man, forty at least.

TWAIN: Thank you.

REPORTER: Where were you born?

TWAIN: In Missouri.

REPORTER: When did you begin to write?

TWAIN: In 1836.

REPORTER: How can that be, if you're only nineteen now?

TWAIN: I don't know.

REPORTER: I want to get something straight before we proceed. What was the date of your birth?

TWAIN: *(Looking the REPORTER straight in the eye)* Monday, October 31st, 1693.

REPORTER: Impossible! That would make you 180 years old.

TWAIN: *(Rising momentarily and shaking the REPORTER'S hand)* You've noticed that! It's always seemed impossible to me, too.

REPORTER: Do you have any brothers or sisters?

TWAIN: Why, now that you remind me of it, yes. I had a brother. William. Bill we called him. Poor old Bill.

REPORTER: Why? Is he dead, then?

TWAIN: Aah! There is a great mystery about that. We could never tell.

REPORTER: *(Nodding his head slowly)* That's sad. Very sad. He disappeared then?

TWAIN: Well, yes, in a general sort of way. *(Pause)* We buried him.

REPORTER: *(Astonished) Buried* him? *Buried* him? Was he dead?

TWAIN: No! no! We only thought he was. See, we were twins, old Bill and me, and we got mixed up in the bathtub when we were infants. One of us drowned. Some think it was Bill, *(Long pause)* others think it was me.

REPORTER: *(Lowering his voice, looking around the room, then back to TWAIN)* What do you think?

Behind the Writing

SAMUEL CLEMENS or MARK TWAIN (1835–1910)

Mark Twain is the pseudonym, or pen name, of Samuel Clemens. Clemens grew up in Hannibal, Missouri. He was fascinated by the steamboats that passed Hannibal on the Mississippi River. *Mark twain* is a phrase that was used by steamboat crew members to indicate the depth of the water.

Two of Twain's most beloved novels are *The Adventures of Tom Sawyer* (1876) and *The Adventures of Huckleberry Finn* (1884).

TWAIN: Why, I'd give anything to know! It is a puzzle, wouldn't you agree? *(Rising and moving toward the REPORTER)* This has been quite pleasant. I'm sorry you must go. May I show you out? *(Slapping the REPORTER on the back and hurrying him toward the door)* Best of luck, and should you run into Bill, give him my warmest regards.

(The dazed REPORTER scratches his head, pauses for a moment in the open door, and backs out slowly. TWAIN shuts the door, pushes his back against it and smiles broadly.)

(Stage lights dim)

(Curtain)

1. The setting of this scene is described as

   A. Mark Twain's front porch.
   B. a hotel room in the Midwest.
   C. a rooming house in Hannibal, Missouri.
   D. a theater in which Twain is to speak.

2. Read the following sentence.

   Mark Twain decides to have a little fun with a reporter who asks the same questions he has answered hundreds of times.

   This sentence best describes the play's

   A. plot.
   B. narrator.
   C. setting.
   D. stage directions.

3. The author shows stage directions by putting them in parentheses and

   A. italic letters.
   B. capital letters.
   C. bold-faced letters.
   D. underlined letters.

4. Which of these is not a stage prop needed for this play?

   A. a chair
   B. a bed
   C. a bathtub
   D. a notebook

5. Which of the following best describes the reporter?

   A. rude
   B. bored
   C. confused
   D. angry

6. Which of the following best describes Mark Twain's character in this play?

   A. shy

   B. serious

   C. helpful

   D. playful

7. Read this line from the play.

   > REPORTER: *(Astonished) Buried* him? *Buried* him? Was he dead?

   What does the word *astonished* mean?

   A. delighted

   B. annoyed

   C. amazed

   D. relieved

8. What do Mark Twain's actions in this play tell you about what his personality may have been like? Use details from the play to support your answer.

   _____

   _____

   _____

   _____

   _____

   _____

   _____

   _____

Lesson 8: The Author's Tools

Think about a time when you created something. Perhaps you put together a model airplane, built a robot, or crafted a beaded bracelet. No matter what you made, when you began, you chose the right tools for the job. Some tools, such as pliers or glue, could work for any of these different jobs.

The same is true for authors. Whether they are writing stories, novels, poems, or plays, authors have a set of tools they can use to share their ideas.

In this unit, you've already learned a bit about the language tools poets use, such as figurative language and alliteration. You have also learned about how playwrights use tools such as dialogue and narration. The following tips will give you more information about how authors of all kinds of writing use these and other tools.

 TIP 1: Keep an eye out for descriptive writing.

Descriptive writing tells about a person, place, thing, or action in detail. Good descriptions should keep your interest and attention. They should give enough details that you can "see" for yourself what's being described. Read the following examples:

Example A

> We climbed the trail up the mesa. The wind was blowing strong.

Example B

> The wind blew strong as we climbed the trail, covering the mesa with sand that sifted around our legs and shut out the sky.
>
> —from *Island of the Blue Dolphins* by Scott O'Dell

1. Which description do you think is better? Explain why.

    _____

    _____

    _____

    _____

    _____

TIP 2: Keep an ear out for repetition.

Repetition is a tool in which the author uses the same sound, word, or sentence structure more than once. As you learned in Lesson 6, this form of repetition is also called alliteration. Repeating sounds simply makes the writing more pleasing to the ear, like music. Here is an example of repeating sounds:

> She sells sea shells by the sea shore.

In this example, the consonant sounds "s" and "sh" are repeated. The hissing "s" and "sh" sounds remind the reader of waves crashing and sliding on the beach.

Repeating words or sentence structures helps draw attention to a word or idea. Here is an example of repeating words:

> How much wood would a woodchuck chuck if a woodchuck could chuck wood?

Notice that the words *wood*, *would*, and *chuck* are repeated. In this case, the repetition is for fun. It draws attention to the word, *woodchuck*. (In fact, a woodchuck doesn't toss wood at all; it burrows in the soil. That's why its other name is *groundhog*.)

Here is an example of repeating sentence structure:

> I came; I saw; I conquered.

In this case, the word *I* is repeated, followed by a verb. The repetition emphasizes the idea that the speaker did what he did (conquer) quickly, deliberately, and without much effort.

2. What kind of repetition is used in the following passage?

> Young Booker was not alone. As slaves, his people had not been allowed to read or write. Now that they were free, everyone in his town wanted to learn. There were night schools, day schools, and Sunday schools. Young and old alike attended.

   A. repetition of sentences

   B. repetition of sentence structures

   C. repetition of sounds

   D. repetition of words

3. What effect does this repetition have on the passage?

_____

_____

_____

_____

 TIP 3: Keep track of dialogue.

Dialogue is the speech of the characters or people in a piece of writing. Dialogue is usually shown in quotation marks (" "). Authors often use dialogue to make their writing more interesting. The characters' words help show what kind of people they are. Dialogue can also work to move the plot along.

Writers tend to follow certain rules in writing dialogue. These rules help you keep track of who is saying what.

- The words inside the quotation marks tell what the character says.

- The words outside the quotation marks tell which character says the dialogue and may even describe how the character says it. (Sometimes, the author does not give this information directly. If it is obvious who is talking, there may be no information outside the quotation marks.)

- When the speaker changes, the author starts a new paragraph.

Read the following piece of dialogue. As you can tell from the first line, it is set in a classroom. The teacher is asking questions about a story the students have just read. If this story is well written, the dialogue will serve a purpose. It will tell us something about the people doing the talking.

> The teacher's voice broke up Booker's daydreaming. "What does this character do to deserve his fate?"
>
> The girl next to Booker replied, "He tries to cheat."
>
> "Very good," replied the teacher. "He tries to get around the rules. Why is cheating wrong?"
>
> Booker spoke up. "It makes you an untrustworthy person."
>
> "Very good, Booker. Does everybody know the word *trustworthy*? It's very much just what it says, 'worthy of trust' . . ."

4. Who speaks in the first paragraph?

   A. a girl

   B. Booker

   C. the teacher

   D. a character in the story Booker read

5. Who speaks in the second paragraph?

   A. a girl

   B. the teacher

   C. Booker

   D. a character in the story Booker read

6. How many people speak in this passage?

   A. two

   B. three

   C. four

   D. five

The following passage is a fictional retelling of an event in the life of Booker T. Washington. Washington was an important American educator. Read the passage. It will be used to help you understand the tips in this lesson.

Booker T. Gets in a Jam

by Greta Anderson

Booker finished reading the story his teacher had assigned and gazed up at the clock in the log cabin where he and the other black children of Malden went to school. He gazed with a gaze that was, perhaps, different from the others'. He willed the hands to stay where they were. After school, he would have to go to work at the salt mine. He had no choice; his family needed his wages.

The black man who taught them was from Ohio, the North. He reminded Booker a lot of the very first black man he had met who could read. Booker could still see him. The man was just a boy, really—a boy surrounded by the men and women of the West Virginia mining town as he read the newspaper to them. Booker had vowed then and there to get an education.

Young Booker was not alone. As slaves, his people had not been allowed to read or write. Now that they were free, everyone in his town wanted to learn. There were night schools, day schools, and Sunday schools. Young and old alike attended, and all the black families gave a bit of money to pay the teacher's salary. Booker liked to think that the money he made packing salt went straight to supporting the school.

The teacher's voice broke up his daydreaming. "What does this character do to deserve his fate?"

The girl next to Booker replied, "He tries to cheat."

"Very good," replied the teacher. "He tries to get around the rules. Why is cheating wrong?"

Booker spoke up. "It makes you an untrustworthy person."

"Very good, Booker. Does everybody know the word *trustworthy*? It's very much just what it says, 'worthy of trust' . . ."

As the teacher explained the word and wrote it on the blackboard, Booker looked back up at the clock and felt his stomach tighten. It would be only half an hour before he would have to leave for work. When he got to work he might have to face the results of what he had done that morning.

Booker had started off going to night school, after his shift at the mine was over. But he wanted to go to school with the other kids his age, and he begged his stepfather to let him. Finally, his stepfather talked to the boss. If Booker arrived at work by 6 A.M., he could leave at 9 A.M., when school started. Then, he would return to the job after school was over.

Booker T. Washington was born a slave in Virginia, in 1856. He was nine years old when the Civil War ended and slaves gained their freedom. His family moved to West Virginia, where he looked for an education. He always believed that education, hard work, and honesty were the keys to success for himself and his people. After attending and later teaching at an industrial school in Virginia, Washington founded an African-American school in Alabama called Tuskegee Institute. With Booker leading it, Tuskegee became famous for developing the talents of many young African Americans, including the famous inventor George Washington Carver.

There was just one problem. His job was two miles from school. No matter how fast he ran the distance, Booker was always late to school. He hated the way all eyes turned when he entered, not to mention the disapproving look on the teacher's face.

This morning, he had solved the problem. As he worked, Booker kept one eye on the clock in the office and the other eye on his boss. When the big hand and the little hand lined up at 8:43, Booker left his post, dashed over to the office and moved the hands so that the clock read "9:00." He put on his cap and found the boss.

"Time to go," he said.

"See you this afternoon," said his boss.

And Booker left for school. Today, he had been on time. Today, he had gotten the chance to read his homework out loud. Today, the teacher had nodded his approval.

Booker's eyes returned to the word on the board.

Untrustworthy. Did it apply to him?

His stomach tightened again as the clock's big hand inched forward.

A Matter of Time

If this story were just about what happens in the present, there would not be much to it. Booker looks at the clock, answers a question, and looks back at the clock. The hands on the clock inch forward.

But the story is not just about what goes on in the classroom. It is also about the conflict Booker feels between being a good student and being a good worker. Remember that conflict is a problem or problems between two or more people or situations. In this situation, he cannot be both. To develop the conflict, the author gives background information, flashbacks, and foreshadowing. **Background information** is a summary of events that happened in the past. **Flashbacks** take the reader to a scene from the past. **Foreshadowing** is when the writer suggests what will happen in the future. The following tips will help you learn about these three writing techniques.

TIP 4: Pay attention to background information.

When the author explains part of the history of the slaves in the South, this background information helps us understand why Booker is so eager to go to school. Likewise, the information about Booker's schedule helps us understand why he changes the clock.

7. Why do Booker and others like him want to learn to read and write?

    A. They would rather work for the newspaper than in the salt mines.

    B. They need to learn to read and write in order to escape to the North.

    C. When they were slaves, they weren't allowed to read and write.

    D. They would like to become teachers like the man from Ohio.

8. Why does Booker move the clock forward at work?

    A. He is getting back at his stepfather.

    B. He wants to get to school on time.

    C. He does not like his job.

    D. He wants to see what he can get away with.

 TIP 5: Flashbacks show what happened in the past.

Flashbacks are like background information, with one difference. Flashbacks take us back to the past, setting a scene that we can "see" with our mind's eye. Sometimes flashbacks include dialogue. They can last for a paragraph or for several pages. The difference between flashbacks and background information is the difference between showing and telling.

9. Which of these sentences from the first half of the passage shows the beginning of a flashback?

    A. Booker could still see him.

    B. Booker had vowed then and there to get an education.

    C. The teacher's voice broke up his daydreaming.

    D. Booker spoke up.

10. At the end of the passage, what occurs in the flashback that concludes with Booker looking at the word on the board?

_____

_____

_____

_____

 TIP 6: Foreshadowing gives clues about the future.

As a reader, you might think that Booker cannot get away with what he is doing for very long. As a careful reader, you know that he can't. That's because the author uses foreshadowing. Foreshadowing is simply a hint about the future. When the author writes that Booker might have to face the consequences of his actions, she is using foreshadowing.

11. The passage says that Booker's stomach tightens when he looks at the clock. The author gives this detail in order to show that Booker

A. had to skip breakfast to go to school.

B. is hoping he'll have time to answer more questions.

C. is looking forward to going back to work.

D. fears he will have to answer for what he did at work.

Other Choices

You've learned about several tools authors use in their writing. These are only a few of the choices authors make, however. If a dozen writers were all given the same topic, all of them would write about that topic in a different way. As you read, think about the choices the author made and how they affect the writing. Ask yourself, *Why did the author write this in this way?*

TIP 7: Notice how the genre affects the meaning of the passage.

Perhaps the most important choice an author makes is about what type of writing to do in the first place. The author of "Booker T. Gets in a Jam" chose to turn an actual event into a fictional story. The following paragraph from Washington's autobiography describes the actual event. An autobiography is a story that a writer tells about him- or herself.

from

Up From Slavery

by Booker T. Washington

The schoolhouse was some distance from the [salt] furnace, and as I had to work till nine o'clock, and the school opened at nine, I found myself in a difficulty. School would always be begun before I reached it, and sometimes my class had recited. To get around this difficulty I yielded to a temptation for which most people, I suppose, will condemn me; but since this is a fact, I might as well state it. . . . There was a large clock in a little office in the furnace. This clock, of course, all the hundred or more workmen depended upon to regulate their hours of beginning and ending the day's work. I got the idea that the way for me to reach school on time was to move the clock hands from half-past eight up to the nine o'clock mark. This I found myself doing morning after morning, till the furnace "boss" discovered that something was wrong, and locked the clock in a case. I did not mean to inconvenience anybody. I simply meant to reach that schoolhouse in time.

12. What are some ways in which "Booker T. Gets in a Jam" differs from this passage from *Up From Slavery*?

_____

_____

_____

_____

13. What effect does the fictional story have that the autobiography does not?

   A. It gives more details about what the boss and other workmen at the mine thought about Booker changing the clock.

   B. It helps the reader hear more of what Booker thought about school in his own words.

   C. It helps the reader more fully imagine the worry and guilt Booker might have felt about changing the clock.

   D. It helps the reader clearly picture what type of work Booker did every day at the mine.

 TIP 8: Notice elements that make up the author's style.

An author's **style** is the way he or she writes. Does the author use simple words or difficult words? Are the sentences long or short? Does the speed of the writing seem slow or fast? What kinds of rhythms do the words create? Does the author use standard English or a form of slang—or both? How does the author try to grab and hold your attention? Notice how choices such as these affect the writing—and you.

Reading Practice

Directions: Read the passage and answer the questions that follow.

from

Annie John

by Jamaica Kincaid

One day, I was throwing stones at a guava tree, trying to knock down a ripe guava, when the Red Girl came along and said, "Which one do you want?" After I pointed it out, she climbed up the tree, picked the one I wanted off its branch, climbed down, and presented it to me. How my eyes did widen and my mouth form an "o" at this. I had never seen a girl do this before. All the boys climbed trees for the fruit they wanted, and all the girls threw stones to knock the fruit off the trees. But look at the way she climbed that tree: better than any boy.

Polishing off the delicious ripe-to-perfection guava in two bites, I took a good look at the Red Girl. How right I had been to take some special notice of her the first time I had seen her. She was holding on to her mother's skirt and I was holding on to my mother's skirt. Our mothers waved to each other as they passed, calling out the usual greetings, making the usual inquiries. I noticed that the girl's hair was the color of a penny fresh from the mint, and that it was so unruly it had to be forcibly twisted into corkscrews, the ends tied tightly with white thread. The corkscrews didn't lie flat on her head, they stood straight up, and when she walked they bounced up and down as if they were something amphibian[1] and alive. Right away to myself I called her the Red Girl. For as she passed, in my mind's eye I could see her surrounded by flames, the house she lived in on fire, and she could not escape. I rescued her, and after that she followed me around worshipfully and took with great forbearance[2] any and every abuse I heaped on her. I would have gone on like that for a while, but my mother tugged at me, claiming my attention; I heard her say, "Such a nice woman, to keep that girl so dirty."

The Red Girl and I stood under the guava tree looking each other up and down. What a beautiful thing I saw standing before me. Her face was big and round and red, like a moon— a red moon. She had big, broad, flat feet, and they were naked to the bare ground; her dress was dirty, the skirt and blouse tearing away from each other at one side; the red hair that I

---

[1] **amphibian:** a class of animals including frogs, toads, newts, and salamanders

[2] **forbearance:** means patience

had first seen standing up on her head was matted and tangled; her hands were big and fat, and her fingernails held at least ten anthills of dirt under them. And on top of that, she had such an unbelievable, wonderful smell, as if she had never taken a bath in her whole life.

I soon learned this about her: She took a bath only once a week, and that was only so that she could be admitted to her grandmother's presence. She didn't like to bathe, and her mother didn't force her. She changed her dress once a week for the same reason. She preferred to wear a dress until it just couldn't be worn anymore. Her mother didn't mind that, either. She didn't like to comb her hair, though on the first day of school she could put herself out for that. She didn't like to go to Sunday school, and her mother didn't force her. She didn't like to brush her teeth, but occasionally her mother said it was necessary. She loved to play marbles, and was so good that only the Skerritt boys now played against her. Oh, what an angel she was, and what a heaven she lived in! I, on the other hand, took a full bath every morning and a sponge bath every night. I could hardly go out on my doorstep without putting my shoes on. I was not allowed to play in the sun without a hat on my head. My mother paid a woman who lived five houses away from us sevenpence a week—a penny for each school day and twopence for Sunday—to comb my hair. On Saturday, my mother washed my hair. Before I went to sleep at night, I had to make sure my uniform was clean and creaseless and all laid out for the next day. I had to make sure that my shoes were clean and polished to a nice shine. I went to Sunday school every Sunday unless I was sick. I was not allowed to play marbles, and, as for the Skerritt boys, that was hardly mentionable.

Behind the Writing

JAMAICA KINCAID
(1949–)

Jamaica Kincaid was born on the tiny Caribbean island of Antigua, then moved to New York City as an adult. Many of her books are about her island and its people's history. In colonial times, the Caribbean Islands had a large population of African slaves working on Spanish, French, or English sugar plantations. Many people from the Caribbean, including Kincaid, have a mixed ancestry.

---

1. What kind of background information does the author provide in the first paragraph?

   A. a description of how the Red Girl bathes

   B. an explanation of the usual roles of boys and girls in the story's setting

   C. an explanation of the narrator's thoughts about her mother

   D. a description of what the narrator would do if the Red Girl's house were on fire

2. Which line from the second paragraph signals the beginning of a flashback?

   A. How right I had been to take some special notice of her the first time I had seen her.

   B. I noticed that the girl's hair was the color of a penny fresh from the mint . . .

   C. Right away to myself I called her the Red Girl.

   D. I would have gone on like that for a while, but my mother tugged at me, claiming my attention . . .

3. From whose point of view is the story told?

   A. a girl's

   B. the Red Girl's

   C. a mother's

   D. an outside narrator's

4. Which of the following techniques is used most in the third paragraph?

   A. dialogue

   B. foreshadowing

   C. description

   D. flashback

5. Which word best characterizes the Red Girl?

   A. graceful

   B. mean

   C. silly

   D. free

6. Read the following line from the story:

   > Her face was big and round and red, like a moon—a red moon.

   This line contains what type of figurative language?

   A. a simile

   B. a metaphor

   C. hyperbole

   D. personification

7. The third paragraph says that the Red Girl's "fingernails held at least ten anthills of dirt under them." Why does the author use this hyperbole?

   A. to compare the girl to an insect

   B. to give human-like qualities to the ants

   C. to show how dirty the girl's fingers are

   D. to show that the girl enjoys anthills

8. If the author had written a play instead of a story, how would the writing most likely be different? Use details from the story to support your answer.

_____

_____

_____

_____

_____

_____

_____

_____

_____

Critical Thinking Skills

Do you enjoy building things? Or do you prefer taking things apart to see how they work? In this unit, you will practice putting together ideas to build meaning. You'll also practice taking apart, or **analyzing**, a piece of writing to see how it works. You'll learn how to determine the author's purpose for writing. You'll practice applying what you learn from your reading to your own life. Lastly, you'll review ways to go beyond a single author's work to find out more about a topic.

In This Unit

Making Connections

The Author's Purpose

Applying What You Read

Finding Out More

Lesson 9: Making Connections

Imagine that you are reading a story that includes the following details.

The butler, Simon, has been treated badly by his employer, the rich and snooty Miss Maple. He knows she has a terrible secret: She stole a million dollars from the bank where she used to work. He tells her that he intends to turn her in to the authorities, but in a nasty scene she throws him out of the house. Now Miss Maple has disappeared. So has her jewelry. So has Simon.

Did Simon kidnap Miss Maple? Did the two of them run away to Brazil together? Did Miss Maple pay Simon off and go into hiding? Or did something else happen? How can you find out?

Putting the Pieces Together

As you continue to read the story about Simon and Miss Maple, you pick up a lot of little details. You find out what kind of people the main characters are. You also learn to predict their actions in different circumstances.

You learn that Miss Maple has been mean to Simon. Simon has tried for years to get her to give him a raise. You come to the conclusion that Simon and Miss Maple would *never* run off together. After all, they don't even *like* each other.

You don't know everything about Miss Maple and Simon, but you do know some things. You can make some pretty good guesses about what happened to both of them. **Inferences** are guesses based on known facts.

You know that Simon has always been honest. His actions in the story show that he believes in doing what's right. **Inferences** are connections between ideas that you make on your own. You can infer that Simon isn't the kind of guy who would kidnap Miss Maple—or anyone else. You can also infer that he wouldn't let Miss Maple pay him off.

A **conclusion** is something you judge to be true. You put together your inferences to come up with the conclusion that something terrible has happened to Simon. You'd have to read the rest of the story to find out whether your inferences and conclusion were correct.

In this lesson, you will learn how to make good inferences—ones that are likely to be correct. You'll also practice making some specific types of inferences: comparing and contrasting, figuring out causes and effects, and looking at problems and finding solutions.

Read the following passage. It will be used to help you understand the tips in this lesson.

Friend Against Friend
by Anne Elliot

The Civil War (1861–1865) divided not only the nation, but friends and families as well. When the Southern states declared their independence, soldiers from the South had to choose whether to be loyal to the Union or to their home states. The passage that follows is about how the war separated two friends but didn't destroy their friendship.

On a spring night in 1861, a small party took place at an army post in Los Angeles (which was just a small town at that time). In many ways, it was just an ordinary party: People played music, sang songs, told jokes, and talked about the good times they had enjoyed together. But this party was different from most. In a few weeks, the people laughing together at this party would be fighting a war against each other.

The people at the party were army officers and their wives. For many years, these officers had served together in the United States Army. Now, the United States was splitting apart. The Civil War had just begun, and therefore many of the officers from Southern states had chosen to go home and serve in the Confederate army. Their friends who would be fighting for the North decided to throw them a farewell party.

It was hard for the officers to say good-bye, especially for Captain Lewis Armistead and Major Winfield Hancock. Armistead was from Virginia, Hancock from Pennsylvania. That had never been an issue before. They had been close friends for more than 15 years. At first, it had seemed unlikely that these two men would be friends because they were so different. Armistead was several years older than Hancock and considered himself a Southern gentleman. Unlike Armistead, the younger Hancock had a reputation as a person who loved parties, eating, dancing, and talking. He often teased Armistead the way a boy might tease his big brother.

Lewis Armistead

Winfield Hancock

But over the years, the two friends went through tough times together. They both fought in the Mexican War, and Hancock had comforted Armistead when Armistead lost his wife and child to illness. These things brought the friends closer together as they grew older. Armistead and Hancock became almost like family to each other.

But now they would be separated, maybe for years, maybe forever. Armistead would be serving in the Confederate army; Hancock would fight on the side of the Union. In a tearful good-bye, Armistead gave his old friend a new major's uniform and gave Hancock's wife, Almira, his personal prayer book. Armistead said he wished God would strike him down if he ever attacked Hancock. Both men hoped they never would have to fight against each other.

Their hope stayed alive for more than two years. Hancock and Armistead were involved in many battles, and each did well. The two friends were both promoted to general. But they had never faced each other in the same battle. All that changed, however, one hot summer day.

The Battle of Gettysburg took place on July 1–3, 1863. It was the best chance the South had to win the war. For the first two days, the fighting was fierce, but neither side could claim victory. On July 3, the Confederates tried one last time. They decided to charge the Northern position, hoping to break through and win the battle. One of the leaders of this charge was Lewis Armistead. He knew that the man commanding the Northern troops across from him was his old friend, Winfield Hancock.

Armistead hated the idea of fighting his friend, but he had been ordered to help lead the charge. He and his men, along with thousands of other Southern troops, formed a line more than a mile long and got ready to head toward the Northern position. Armistead placed his black felt hat on his sword and held it up to guide his troops forward through the smoke and confusion of the battle.

Slowly, the long line started walking across an open field toward the enemy. Soon, the Northern guns started to take their toll. The Southern soldiers moved more quickly, but they continued to lose men with every step. Finally, Armistead and a small number of his troops reached the Northern lines. With his black hat still on his sword, he captured a Northern cannon. Just as he did, however, he was shot. He fell to the ground wounded, and the rest of his men were captured or forced to retreat.

When Armistead was found by one of Hancock's officers, he had a message for his old friend. He said, "Tell General Hancock from me, that I have done him and you all a grave injustice."

As it turned out, Hancock had been wounded at almost the same moment that Armistead had. Both of the friends were hurt badly, but doctors thought each would survive. Hancock did get better, but Armistead died two days after being wounded.

While Lewis Armistead and Winfield Hancock never saw each other face to face after that night in Los Angeles, it's clear from Armistead's last words to Hancock that their friendship had survived one of the most terrible battles of the Civil War. Even a war that divided country, families, and friends could not destroy the friendship between these men.

 TIP 1: Put together details from the passage to make inferences.

To **infer** means to figure out something beyond what is stated in the passage. Inferences require you to "read between the lines" and go beyond what is stated. Good inferences are reasonable and are based on details in the passage. Often, all you need to do is add up the details to make an inference.

1. What was the main reason that Armistead and Hancock's goodbye in Los Angeles was tearful?

   A. Armistead gave his personal prayer book to Hancock's wife.

   B. The close friends were parting to fight on opposite sides in a war.

   C. Armistead was thinking back to when he lost his wife and child to illness.

   D. The men talked about the times they spent together in the Mexican War.

2. How do you know? Underline details in the passage that support your answer to Number 1.

Sometimes, you may need to make an inference based on a generalization. A **generalization** is a broad statement that applies to more than one specific situation. For example, you could make this generalization: When people cry, it is often because they are sad about something. You can use this general idea to help you answer Number 1. What were the biggest reasons Armistead and Hancock had for being sad on that night?

For some test questions, you may also need to do this in reverse, and choose a general statement based on specific details in a passage. When asked to pick a generalization about a passage, look for a general statement that holds true for all of the specific examples in the passage.

3. Which of the following generalizations can you make based on the passage?

   A. During the Civil War, many friends had to fight on opposite sides.

   B. During the Civil War, many battles took place in Gettysburg.

   C. During the Civil War, many soldiers gave away their prayer books.

   D. During the Civil War, many men lost their wives to illness.

TIP 2: Make sure your inferences and conclusions are supported by evidence from the passage.

Evidence is proof that shows what you or someone else says is correct. Whenever you make an inference, your answer must be supported by evidence from the passage. The answers to inference questions aren't stated directly in the passage. They are supported, however, by something in the passage: details, the author's tone, foreshadowing and so on. You should be able to point directly to a place in the passage that supports any statement you make about a story or article.

4. Which statement best describes Armistead and Hancock's friendship?

   A. It was strong because of the difficulties the men shared.

   B. It was strong because the two men were so much alike.

   C. It was weak because the two men teased each other often.

   D. It wasn't likely to last because the men were from two different states.

5. How do you know the answer to Number 4? Underline details in the passage that support your answer to Number 4.

Here are a few more questions that will help you practice looking for supporting evidence.

6. Which conclusion is best supported by the information in the passage?

   A. Armistead wanted Hancock to fight on the side of the South.

   B. Neither man believed that a civil war should be fought over slavery.

   C. The men would not have been as close had they both been from the same region.

   D. Going through hard times together helped Armistead and Hancock grow closer.

7. Which statement about Hancock is best supported by the passage?

   A. He allowed himself to be wounded on purpose.

   B. He was an outgoing person who liked to have fun.

   C. He did not feel as strongly about the friendship as Armistead did.

   D. He was angry that he had to go to war against the South.

8. The author concludes that Hancock and Armistead's friendship survived one of the most terrible battles of the Civil War. Which of the following is the best evidence for this conclusion?

   A. Hancock was wounded at almost the same time Armistead was.

   B. Armistead led Confederate troops against Hancock's Union troops.

   C. Armistead's men were captured or forced to retreat at the end of the battle.

   D. Armistead sent a message of apology to Hancock after he was wounded.

Predictions are guesses about what might happen. Predictions also need to be supported by evidence from the passage.

9. What would most likely have happened if Armistead had not been ordered to lead the charge against Hancock's troops?

   A. Hancock would not have survived the battle.

   B. Hancock's troops would have lost the battle.

   C. Armistead would not have fought against his friend.

   D. Armistead would have left the military after the battle.

10. How do you know?

   _____

   _____

11. What did Armistead mean by saying he had done Hancock and his troops "a grave injustice"?

   A. Armistead had acted wrongly toward them.

   B. Armistead had chosen the wrong battle plan.

   C. Armistead had not expected to be wounded.

   D. Armistead had hoped to be more successful.

12. Which of the following best describes Armistead?

   A. uncaring

   B. grown-up

   C. jolly

   D. wild

Alike and Different

You can use your inference skills to compare and contrast ideas in a passage. To **compare** means to show how two or more things are alike and different. To **contrast** means to focus mainly on the differences between things. The following tips will help you practice making comparisons and contrasts.

 TIP 3: Look for words or phrases that show comparisons.

Authors will often tell you when they are making a comparison. By using words and phrases that let you know a comparison is coming, authors clearly show when they want you to see how two things are alike or different. These comparisons are usually easy to find—locate the word or phrase, and you've found the comparison.

For example, imagine you're reading a passage about animals that sleep during the day and are active at night. The author might compare night-time animals to day-time animals, animals that sleep at night, by saying something like this:

> **Both** night-time animals (such as owls) and day-time animals (such as hawks) can have very sharp vision. **However**, night-time animals, including owls, usually have much larger eyes that are better for seeing in the dark.

The author uses the words *both* and *however* to clearly show when a comparison is coming.

The list below gives just a few examples of words that let you know an author is comparing or contrasting.

Words that show similarities:

alike	also	as well as	both	just as
like	similar	same	too	together

Words that show differences:

but	different	even though	except
however	instead	not	not like
though	unlike	on the other hand	whereas

13. Go back to "Friend Against Friend" and circle any words or phrases that show similarities or differences.

14. What is one way in which Armistead and Hancock were alike?

   A. Both lost a child to illness.

   B. Both fought in the Mexican War.

   C. Neither wanted to serve in the Confederate Army.

   D. Neither wanted a career in the military.

 TIP 4: Look for details that show comparisons.

Not all comparisons are as clearly stated as the examples in the last tip. Sometimes you may be asked to put details together in order to tell how things, characters, or events are different or alike.

For example, let's return to the passage about night-time animals. Suppose that, instead of comparing them in the same paragraph, the author describes the hawk and the owl in two separate paragraphs. Each paragraph includes details about each bird's vision and eye size. The author does not come right out and tell you how they are alike and different. You will have to look at these details together to make the comparison.

15. In the following table, list details from the passage that describe Armistead and Hancock.

Armistead	Hancock

16. What is one way in which Armistead and Hancock were different?

A. Armistead was younger than Hancock.

B. Armistead was married and Hancock was not married.

C. Armistead lived a quieter life than Hancock.

D. Armistead fought for the Union, Hancock for the Confederacy.

TIP 5: Make your own comparisons.

Sometimes you'll be asked to compare two things in a more general way. A single detail won't be enough. You'll need to put together several details to come up with a bigger picture and make a comparison. Try this on the following question.

17. Which of the following words best describes both Lewis Armistead and Winfield Hancock?

    A. cruel

    B. quiet

    C. serious

    D. thoughtless

Causes and Effects

Many stories and articles try to explain how or why something happened. That's why reading material is often filled with causes and effects. The following tips will help you examine causes and effects in a reading passage.

 TIP 6: Look for words that show causes and effects.

Certain words are direct clues to cause-and-effect relationships. Spotting these words can help you notice causes and effects in the things you read. Here is a list of cause and effect words to watch for.

Cause/Effect Words

caused by	in order to	led to	since
due to	in response to	because	for this reason
therefore	so	as a result	was responsible for

18. Go back to the passage and reread the first three paragraphs. Draw a box around any words or phrases that show causes or effects.

19. Why did many of the U.S. Army officers from Southern states go home to serve in the Confederate Army?

    A. They were needed to fight in the Civil War.

    B. They no longer had friends in the North.

    C. The Mexican War was a bad experience.

    D. They did not like living in California.

20. According to the passage, why was it unlikely at first that Armistead and Hancock would become friends?

    A. They served in different armies.

    B. They disliked each other when they first met.

    C. They seemed to be very different people.

    D. They teased each other too much.

TIP 7: Use the word *because* to connect causes and effects.

Sometimes causes and effects are implied rather than directly stated. You will need to make your own connections in these cases. The most important connecting word is *because*.

21. In paragraph 6 of the passage, the author says, "The two friends were both promoted to general." Use what you know from the passage to complete the following sentence.

    The two friends were both promoted to general *because*

    _____

    _____

    _____

Now use your "because" sentence to help you answer the following multiple-choice question.

22. The two friends were both promoted to general because they

    A. were seriously wounded in battle.

    B. led their troops well in many battles.

    C. never faced each other in the same battle.

    D. led their troops in the Battle of Gettysburg.

Problems and Solutions

Many passages center around some sort of problem. In a fictional story, the characters try to solve the problem. In nonfiction passages, authors often describe how people have faced difficult problems in our world. In some cases, the author may present a current problem, along with a potential solution and reasons to support it.

 TIP 8: Good solutions address the cause of the problem, as well as the effects.

Imagine that you have accidentally burned your hand on your oven door while baking cookies. One solution to the problem of your burned hand is to apply first aid. But how will you avoid burning your hand again?

In looking at problems and solutions, it is important to first look at the *causes* of the problem: touching a hot oven door will cause a person to get burned. A good solution will often address the cause, not just the effects, of the problem: perhaps you need to use an oven mitt the next time you decide to bake cookies.

Let's look at the problems facing Armistead and Hancock in "Friend Against Friend."

23. What was the main problem that Armistead and Hancock faced?

    A. They feared they might have to fight against each other.

    B. They were not as skilled at war as they needed to be.

    C. They did not agree on the issues that caused the war.

    D. They did not have very much in common.

24. What was the cause of their problem?

    A. They had just finished fighting in the Mexican War.

    B. They served together as officers in the United States Army.

    C. They were military men serving on opposite sides in a war.

    D. Hancock lived a wild life, whereas Armistead was a gentleman.

25. How did Armistead try to deal with the problem?

    A. He allowed himself to become wounded in battle.

    B. He offered to adopt Hancock as his own son.

    C. He disobeyed orders given by his superiors.

    D. He swore he would never attack Hancock in a battle.

TIP 9: Proposed solutions should be supported by good reasons.

In some passages, an author will describe a problem and offer a possible solution. When an author suggests a solution to a problem, notice whether the idea is supported by strong reasons. Does the solution seem realistic? Do the reasons the author gives to support the solution seem reasonable?

In Lesson 10, you will learn more about evaluating an author's reasoning.

Find the Connection

Everything you read can tell you something about the world. Articles about historic people and events can give you an idea of what life was like many years ago. Essays about other lands can teach you about how people in other countries live. Sometimes, even fictional stories can give you an understanding about real life.

 TIP 10: Use connection strategies to learn what the text says about the world.

Throughout this lesson, you have learned strategies for making different kinds of connections as you read. You can use these same strategies to learn how to connect different texts to real life.

Sometimes you can find these messages easily, but other times you have to look harder. Use the connection strategies you learned in this lesson to find these messages. Connecting what you read with the real world can make your reading experience more meaningful.

26. Go back to the passage and number each piece of information that tells you what life was like in America during the Civil War.

27. In what ways is life in America different today than it was in Lewis Armistead and Winfield Hancock's time?

_____

_____

_____

_____

_____

Reading Practice

Directions: Read the passage and answer the questions that follow.

Pick It Up!

by Linda Massey

Many people think that litter is unsightly, but until recently, few people did anything about it. Read on to learn about the volunteers who pick up litter along our highways.

In some places, the trash on our roadsides is enough to make a person cry. All 50 states have tried many ways to reduce littering, from fines to television advertisements. One idea that is quickly catching on is "adopt a highway."

The idea began in Tyler, Texas, with Bobby Evans, a highway official who hates litter. Mr. Evans persuaded several groups in East Texas to clean up roadsides. The highway department agreed to put up two large signs with a group's name on them—one at each end of a two-mile stretch of road. Four times a year, group members put on orange vests and pick up trash along that road—bags and bags of it.

Tyler's Civitan Club was the first to volunteer, but soon people were helping throughout Texas. A Louisiana state senator saw the signs and convinced the people in his state to start a program of their own. The idea rapidly spread across the nation.

A woman in Idaho patrols 16 miles of Highway 95. In 1991, dressed in a floppy hat, gloves, and boots, Virginia Prieber picked up more than 2,300 pounds of trash all by herself. She got so mad about the trash that once she sent some back to its owner! She found a bag of trash with the owner's name and address inside, so she packaged it up and mailed it to him first class.

Adopt-a-Highway Programs

Adopt-a-Highway programs save taxpayers clean-up costs. Thousands of groups have adopted miles of roadsides. Each volunteer group agrees to maintain a section of highway, usually removing litter from the area four times a year.

Many types of groups are involved in the program, including schools, businesses, religious organizations, social clubs, and community-service organizations. Some groups use the Adopt-a-Highway program as a fund-raiser. Individuals gather pledges per quarter mile of highway cleaned. All money collected is kept by the participating organization.

Volunteer trash-collection is paying off. It saves states a great deal of money. Clubs, individuals, and families get positive publicity for their efforts. They like having their names appear on the state's roadside signs. Most important, however, is the effect the program has on littering. People who spend the day getting dirty while picking up trash are less likely to litter themselves. Travelers who see the volunteers working will perhaps think twice before littering.

Wouldn't you like to get involved, too? It's easy. Just contact your state highway department and ask for more information. See you on the roadside!

1. What is the main idea of this article?

    A. Virginia Prieber, an Idaho resident, is a super picker-upper.

    B. Citizens and clubs are volunteering to clean up roadsides in several states.

    C. Bobby Evans is the official who first started a highway clean-up project.

    D. States hope that volunteers who pick up trash will not litter.

2. What is the main problem that the Adopt-a-Highway program is meant to address?

    A. how to decrease roadside litter

    B. how to get people to volunteer in their communities

    C. how to get positive publicity for organizations

    D. how to raise money for community groups

3. Read this sentence from the passage.

    All 50 states have tried many ways to <u>reduce</u> littering, from fines to television advertisements.

    What does the word *reduce* mean?

    A. to throw away

    B. to decrease

    C. to make larger

    D. to clean

4. Which of the following details best supports the main idea of the passage?

    A. Bobby Evans is a highway official in Tyler, Texas.

    B. Group members wear orange vests when they pick up trash.

    C. A Louisiana state senator convinced people to start a program.

    D. Virginia Prieber lives in Idaho near Highway 95.

5. How much trash did Virginia Prieber pick up in 1991?

    A. 23 pounds

    B. 230 pounds

    C. 2,300 pounds

    D. 23,000 pounds

6. Read the following line from the passage:

    Travelers who see the volunteers working will perhaps think twice before littering.

    This means that travelers who see the volunteers may

    A. be less likely to litter.

    B. be more likely to adopt a highway themselves.

    C. wait until they are out of sight to litter.

    D. stop and join the volunteers.

7. The author gives which of the following reasons to support the Adopt-a-Highway idea?

    A. States will compete to have the largest program.

    B. The program earns the states money.

    C. Volunteers are less likely to litter themselves.

    D. Groups dislike the publicity they receive from the signs.

8. What led Virginia Prieber to mail a bag of trash to its owner? Use details from the passage to support your answer.

_____

_____

_____

_____

_____

_____

_____

_____

Lesson 10: The Author's Purpose

Imagine you're shopping at the grocery store. You pass by a stack of bottles filled with a bright pink liquid. In front of the stack is a sign with these words written on it:

> Each eight-ounce serving of NEW Sparkles Soda gives your body the energy it needs every day. Sparkles is sweetened with 100% all-natural sugar, grown in America's heartland. Kids will love the tangy taste and pleasing pink color, but their bodies will love the full day's supply of Vitamin C. And best of all, Sparkles Soda is FAT FREE!

Do you think the person who wrote this is really thinking about how healthy the soda is? Or do you think the author might have another purpose in mind?

You can't see authors' faces or read their body language, and they don't always come right out and tell you what they think or feel. But, you can often tell how they feel by carefully looking at the words they choose. Words are clues that can tell you about authors' reasons for writing, their attitudes toward the subjects they write about, and the effects they want to have on their readers.

The Writer Behind the Writing

An **author's purpose** for writing is why he or she writes. Figuring out an author's purpose is usually just a matter of looking closely at what they have written, and how they wrote it.

Does the author want to scare you? Entertain you? Teach you something? Make you believe something? The tips in this lesson will help you find clues to an author's purpose. They will also help you evaluate an author's ideas so that you can decide whether you agree or disagree with those ideas.

 TIP 1: Notice the author's tone.

When you speak to someone, your tone of voice can tell that person a lot about how you are feeling. If you're upset about something, you might use an angry tone. If you're happy, your tone is probably excited or joyful.

When you read, you can tell a lot about how the author feels about a topic by "listening" to the author's tone. Suppose you are reading a letter from your friend Tamika, who is visiting Morocco. These are the first few sentences of her letter:

> I can't believe I'm here! This country is simply amazing. The marketplace in this town is the busiest, coolest place I think I have ever been. I bought a little wooden monkey there, and it is just adorable!

1. What is Tamika's tone in this part of her letter?

   A. angry

   B. sad

   C. excited

   D. scared

Later in her letter, Tamika's tone changes:

> Although I'm having fun, I have to say I miss you guys a lot. Every night when I'm trying to go to sleep, I think about the people I miss. I wish you could be here with me. It's hard to be in such a faraway place, especially when I don't know anyone here.

2. What is Tamika's tone in this part of her letter?

   A. angry

   B. sad

   C. excited

   D. scared

Try this tip as you read the following passage. Imagine the author is reading the passage to you. Try to "listen" to his voice and figure out his tone as you read.

Read the following passage. It will be used to help you understand the tips in this lesson.

Why I Like Living in a Small Town
by Macon Brisby

This passage is part of an essay written by Macon Brisby for a class assignment. Macon and his family moved from a big city to a small town just over a year ago.

When my parents told me we would be moving to a town with only 3,000 people in it, I have to say, I wasn't very happy. My mom and dad both grew up in small towns, but I had lived all my life in Chicago. *Small towns are boring*, I thought. There wouldn't be anything to do. There would be no malls, no movie theaters, and no big downtown area. I thought the school would be like one of those one-room schoolhouses you see on TV shows about the Old West: no gym, no library, and definitely no computers. I also thought I wouldn't fit in very well in a small town. I figured that everyone there would already know each other. They probably wouldn't want to get to know any new kids.

When we actually moved here, however, I found that I was wrong about small towns. Sure, there aren't as many stores as in the city, but there are a lot more open spaces and fields than I had ever seen in my old neighborhood. This is great for me, since I like playing soccer and baseball more than shopping. The school was a surprise, too. It isn't as big as my old school, but it still has all the same things (including computers). Being in a smaller school also means I get to know my teachers and classmates better than at my old school, which had hundreds of students. I feel like I really belong.

That's probably the best thing about living in a small town: belonging. It turned out that the people here really wanted to get to know us as soon as we got here. Everyone was very friendly, and it wasn't long before most of the people I saw on the street were familiar to me. In the city, most people are strangers, but a small town gives a sense of friendship between the people who live there. It's almost as if everyone in town is your neighbor. You really feel as if you belong to the town and the town belongs to you.

Now answer Numbers 3 and 4 based on the passage you just read.

3. What is the author's tone in most of the passage?

   A. sad
   B. angry
   C. upbeat
   D. funny

4. Underline words or sentences in the passage that support your answer to Number 3.

TIP 2: The author's tone will give hints about his or her attitude.

The author's tone can help you figure out the author's attitude. The author's **attitude** is the way he or she feels about a topic. The author's attitude shows approval or disapproval of the subject.

- A **positive** attitude can show such feelings as happiness, hope, joy, cheerfulness, excitement, or pride.

- A **negative** attitude can show such feelings as sorrow, shame, fear, anger, or boredom.

- A **neutral** attitude doesn't show strong feelings one way or another.

If the author's tone is angry or fearful, the author's attitude is probably negative. If the tone is excited or happy, the attitude is probably positive. If the author doesn't seem to have any strong feelings, the attitude is neutral.

5. What is the author's attitude toward small towns?

   A. mild approval

   B. strong approval

   C. mild disapproval

   D. strong disapproval

 TIP 3: Identify the main idea and the author's viewpoint.

The next step in getting to know the author is to figure out the main idea of the passage.

6. What is this passage mostly about?

   A. Living in a small town has many benefits.

   B. Towns with fewer than 3,000 people usually don't have malls.

   C. Schools in small towns are smaller than schools in cities.

   D. The author's family moved to a small town.

The main idea will be closely linked to the author's viewpoint. Think of **viewpoint** as how the author sees the world. Viewpoint helps give an author an attitude about things. If an author sees the world from the position of a criminal on the run, then that author's attitude towards police might be a negative one.

7. How does the author feel about living in a small town? Support your answer with examples from the passage.

_____

_____

_____

_____

_____

_____

_____

8. What is the author's overall viewpoint in the passage?

   A. Small towns are better and more enjoyable than big cities in every way.

   B. Schools in small towns are not as good as schools in larger cities.

   C. TV programs usually do not show small towns fairly or correctly.

   D. Small towns have much to offer those who choose to live in them.

TIP 4: Determine the author's purpose.

Once you've figured out the author's tone, attitude, main idea, and viewpoint, you should be able to determine the author's reason for writing. What does the author want you to think, feel, or do?

An author's purpose usually falls into one of four major categories:

- **writing to teach or inform** – The author provides factual information in a balanced way. If there are two sides to an issue, the author presents both sides and lets readers draw their own conclusions.

- **writing to persuade** – The author wants to convince the reader to think, believe, or act in a certain way. The author may do this by presenting an argument in favor of certain ideas. The author might also encourage the reader to do something in response to the writing, such as vote for a certain candidate, buy a brand of clothing, or drink a certain brand of soda.

- **writing to entertain** – Some authors just want to entertain their readers—to make them laugh, cry, feel suspense, or otherwise enjoy the writing. Most fiction authors write with this purpose in mind.

- **writing to express** – The author simply wants to pour his or her thoughts and feelings onto paper. Journal entries are one example of this type of writing.

9. What is the author's main purpose in writing "Why I Like Living in a Small Town"?

   A. to express his feelings about his hometown of Chicago

   B. to influence readers to think positively about small towns

   C. to inform readers of ways in which large cities are better than small towns

   D. to entertain readers with funny stories about living in a small town

Examining the Evidence

When you read nonfiction, think about the ideas an author presents. Does the author use good reasoning? Are the ideas supported with facts, explanations, descriptions, examples, details, or other types of evidence? Is the supporting evidence accurate and appropriate? The following tips will help you examine an author's ideas and the evidence for those ideas.

TIP 5: Decide where the writing would most likely appear.

The author's purpose is often linked to the genre he or she is using. Genres allow authors to present their ideas in different ways. For example, if the passage is neutral and filled with information, it might appear in an encyclopedia or a news article. If the passage gives a positive or negative opinion and is intended to persuade readers, it could very well appear in the editorial section of a newspaper or magazine. Here are a few nonfiction genres and their purposes.

- **letters to the editor** – letters that express opinions, often hoping to persuade readers

- **editorials** – columns often written by experts or "insiders" in an attempt to persuade readers to agree with an idea or take some sort of action; editorials tend to base their arguments on both facts and opinions

- **essays** – nonfiction writing that analyzes or interprets a topic or expresses an opinion

- **reviews** – columns or articles describing and expressing an opinion about a performance, exhibit, or work (drama, literature, music, art, etc.)

- **advertisements** – writing that tries to persuade the reader to buy something; advertisements also come in the form of television and radio commercials

 TIP 6: Look out for bias.

One reason we read is to learn about other people's ideas. Sometimes, though, an author's strong feelings about a subject can affect his or her reasoning. The author may see things from only one side, rather than thinking clearly about ALL the facts. This is called having a **bias**.

For example, imagine that your little brother has just seen a new Yu-Gi-Oh! movie. You ask him whether it was any good, and he replies, "Wow! It was awesome—the best movie ever!"

Do you trust his opinion? You remember he said basically the same thing about the last Yu-Gi-Oh! movie. He owns a zillion Yu-Gi-Oh! cards, and Yu-Gi-Oh! posters cover the walls of his room. He even wears Yu-Gi-Oh! pajamas. It is safe to say that your brother has a bias toward all things Yu-Gi-Oh! His opinion of the new Yu-Gi-Oh! movie might not be very trustworthy.

The same is true of what you read. Remember the Sparkle Soda display from the beginning of this lesson? The person who wrote that paragraph probably worked for Sparkle Soda, and wants the Sparkle Soda Company to sell more soda. That person is biased toward Sparkle Soda.

When you read, try to figure out whether the author might have a biased view toward the topic. The following tips will help you spot signs of bias in the things you read.

 TIP 7: Notice which statements are facts and which are opinions.

When evaluating an author's ideas, it is important to be able to tell which statements are facts and which are opinions. Here are a few ways to tell the difference:

Fact Statements:

- **Can be checked.** A fact statement can be checked for accuracy. You can look it up in a reference book or some other source.

- **Use words that have pretty much the same meaning for everyone.** Fact statements are more likely to use words that have meanings everyone can agree on, such as *round, glass, blue, European, wooden, mammal,* or *solid.*

Opinion Statements:

- **Cannot be checked.** An opinion can't be checked for accuracy. Any number of people can have different opinions about the same thing.

- **Use words that mean different things to different people.** Opinion statements often use adjectives such as *beautiful, ugly, frightening, pleasant, expensive,* or *friendly.* They may use nouns such as *superstar* or verbs such as *improve* or *thrill.* An outfit that's *cool* to you may be a *nightmare* to your parents.

The important thing to remember about fact and opinion statements is this: facts say, "Check it out." Opinions say, "Just take my word for it."

Practice Activity

Directions: Write "F" for Fact or "O" for Opinion in front of each statement.

_____ 1. Canada is north of the United States.

_____ 2. Cinco de Mayo is more fun than the Fourth of July.

_____ 3. Babe Ruth hit his first home run on March 7, 1914.

_____ 4. Diamonds are the most beautiful gemstones in the world.

_____ 5. Sally Ride became the first American woman to go into space when she flew on the space shuttle *Challenger*.

_____ 6. Batman is a better superhero than Superman.

_____ 7. Christina Aguilera is the most talented female vocalist performing today.

_____ 8. Christina Aguilera released a Spanish-language CD called *Mi Reflejo*.

_____ 9. The house near the beach is really nice.

_____ 10. There are 31 days in March.

 TIP 8: Look out for bad reasoning.

Imagine that one day your friend said something like this: "Since two multiplied by two equals four, then three multiplied by three must equal six." You would immediately know that this statement was false. It would be obvious that your friend came to the wrong conclusion.

Authors sometimes use bad reasoning that is less obvious than the example above. Even so, if you look closely, you will be able to tell whether the facts "add up" to a sound conclusion. Here are a few common errors in reasoning that you might see:

- **Oversimplifying** makes a complicated issue seem simpler than it really is. Most important issues have many sides to consider.

  It all boils down to this: the key to safe schools is strict discipline.

- **Broad generalization** makes a general statement and applies it across the board, without allowing for any exceptions.

  Kids today watch too much television.

- **Circular reasoning** tries to prove a point by simply rewording it.

  Amala Singh is a great choice for class president because she is perfect for the job.

- **A choice of two extremes** gives only two extreme possibilities without any options in between.

  We must either vote for the new leash law or watch our city go to the dogs.

- **Unsupported judgment** makes a judgment without evidence to support it.

  Despite losing every game this season, I just know that our tennis team will do well in the tournament.

10. The following statement from "Why I Like Living in a Small Town" is best described as which type of bad reasoning?

    Small towns are boring.

    A. circular reasoning
    B. oversimplifying
    C. broad generalization
    D. a choice of two extremes

Bad reasoning can **distort**, or twist, the facts so that they no longer correctly describe the situation. Authors can also twist the facts by using propaganda, as you will see in the following tip.

TIP 9: Beware of propaganda.

Authors sometimes use techniques that are meant to persuade you to act based on your emotions without considering all the facts. This type of reasoning is called **propaganda**. Following are a few of the most commonly used propaganda techniques.

- **Bandwagon effect** suggests that most people support or oppose an issue and asks others to go along with the group.

  But, M-o-m! Everybody else's parents buy their kids Zippy shoes. You should buy me some, too!

- **Name-calling** uses harsh words to describe someone, but doesn't give any facts to support the claims.

  Mr. Wheedle is a big liar.

- **Stereotyping** uses common but unfair images of a group to make a point that isn't true.

  Billy Joe Robbins is one of those spoiled rich kids from Knob Hill, so you know he must get everything he wants.

- **Snobbery** tries to make people think they can be better than others by acting or thinking a certain way.

  Everyone steps aside for people who know what they want in life. Show that you know what you want. Wear Style! cologne.

- **Ordinary folks** tries to connect itself with simple values and down-to-earth people, and says that people who disagree must think they are better than others.

  Hey, I'm your neighbor. We think alike. We know what's right and what's wrong. Those people from Washington are just too high and mighty to understand us country folk.

- **Glittering generalities** uses words that are patriotic, attractive, or catchy but don't really say anything.

  New BLAST detergent gives your clothes Sparkle Power!

- **Scientific claim** attempts to convince readers that a product or idea is scientific and accurate when that may not be the case at all.

  What's said: New, improved CRISPY Natural Oatmeal contains the miracle fiber recommended by most doctors for a healthy diet.

  What's left unsaid: CRISPY Natural Oatmeal contains the same fiber as all other oatmeal.

- **Testimonial** tells you to base your decision on what someone else thinks, usually someone who is famous or important.

    If LeBron O'Jordan recommends these basketball shoes, you know they're the right ones for you!

- **Scare tactics** describes "possible" negative effects with strong and unsupported images that make people act out of fear instead of reason.

    If the people elect Susan Smothers, taxes will go up, crime will skyrocket, and our hometown values will decline!

- **Guilt by association** implies that if you're a friend of a person who did something bad, you are probably guilty, too. (Remember the warning, "You're known by the company you keep"?)

    Felicia hangs around with those kids who broke the school window. She's bound to get in trouble sooner or later, too.

- **Appeal to patriotism** implies that a person is or is not a truly dedicated citizen.

    No true American would ever support the ideas that candidate Williams is proposing.

11. Now try writing some propaganda statements of your own. Choose two propaganda techniques from the list. On the following lines, write a new statement using each technique. You may use words from advertisements or make up your own.

    A. Technique: _____

       Statement: _____

       _____

       _____

    B. Technique: _____

       Statement: _____

       _____

       _____

Remember: If someone tries to persuade you only by stirring your emotions—without backing up his or her ideas with strong evidence—watch out!

TIP 10: Notice hidden messages.

When authors write, they almost always assume that some ideas are true. To **assume** means to believe something without checking it out. They don't bother to support these ideas; they expect their readers to automatically agree with them. In this way, assumed ideas lie under the stated ideas in the passage.

Often, these underlying ideas are things with which nobody would disagree: crime is bad, love is great, helping others is nice. But sometimes an author will slip in an underlying idea that isn't all that clear, or that shows the author's bias. For example, an author who loves to play baseball may assume that all of his or her readers love baseball, too.

When you read, look for underlying messages such as these, and decide for yourself whether you agree with them.

12. What assumption does Macon Brisby make in "Why I Like Living in a Small Town"?

   A. Computers are important for learning.

   B. Shopping is more fun than soccer.

   C. Small towns have the best schools.

   D. Cities are friendlier than small towns.

TIP 11: Evaluate the author's work.

All of the tips you've just reviewed will help you develop an **evaluation**, or overall opinion, of the author's work. When you make an evaluation, you decide whether or not you think the author was successful in his or her purpose. Let's say that you've decided the author's purpose is to persuade you to think or act in a certain way. Should you agree with the author? Before you decide, think about these questions:

• Does the writing have a clear main idea? Does it clearly express the author's position?

• Is the writing helpful for the audience and purpose?

• Is the logic sound? Are the author's conclusions well thought out?

• Is the author's position well supported by relevant facts, details, examples, or other evidence?

• Is the author biased toward or against the subject? Does the author consider other points of view?

• Does the writing distort the facts through the use of bad reasoning or propaganda?

Use the information you gather by thinking about these questions to decide if you think the passage is successful. If the author's purpose is to persuade you, then the passage is only successful if you agree with the author.

You can't very well agree with someone if you don't know exactly what viewpoint you're agreeing with. The first thing you should do when thinking about a persuasive passage is decide what the author's viewpoint is.

13. What is the author's viewpoint in the passage "Why I Like Living in a Small Town"?

    A. Check out the schools when considering a move to a small town.
    B. Small towns are better and more enjoyable than big cities in every way.
    C. TV programs usually do not show small towns fairly or accurately.
    D. There are many reasons to enjoy living in a small town.

Once you have a clear statement of the author's opinion, you should take a look at the facts. Does the author use facts to back up his opinion? Do the facts he uses in the passage support his argument? Could you use other sources to check the facts yourself? Are the facts correct?

14. Write down at least two facts from the passage that provide strong support for the author's opinion. Next to each fact you list, make a check mark if you think you could look the fact up somewhere else to make sure it is correct.

_____

_____

_____

Last, but not least, think about the author's background and personal values. This can help you understand *why* the author wants you to think or act a certain way.

Suppose a letter to the editor in your local newspaper says that people should be allowed to dump old tires in the landfill free of charge. You might notice who wrote the letter to the editor: the owner of a store that sells car tires. You know how much harm tires can cause the environment; why would this store owner want to be able to dump tires more easily? Because it helps the tire store business. Knowing this about the writer, you would be wise to pay careful attention to the facts in the letter to make sure they are accurate and give a balanced picture of the issue.

15. Suppose you were told that the author of "Why I Like Living in a Small Town" was hoping to win a scholarship given to a student from a town of less than 5,000 people. How would this change the way you think about the passage?

_____

_____

_____

TIP 12: Draw your own conclusions.

Reading can help you draw your own conclusions about a topic. The best conclusions are the ones drawn after thinking about all sides of an issue. It is also important to consider the effects of your conclusions. What if everyone felt the way you do—and acted on those feelings?

You might already have an opinion about the topic that the author deals with. Reading other people's viewpoints and reasons, however, can help you think through your own ideas more carefully. You may keep the same opinion you had before, or you might change your opinion when you have more information.

16. Did reading this passage change your opinion about living in a small town or a large city? Why or why not? Support your answer with examples.

_____

_____

_____

_____

_____

_____

_____

_____

Reading Practice

Directions: Read the passage and answer the questions that follow.

The River City Times

Letter to the Editor

What's the point of wearing school uniforms? I'm tired of hearing adults say that uniforms would make kids behave better at school. What I wear doesn't make any difference in how I behave. I'm me, and I'll act like I think I should no matter what I wear. Whether I'm in jeans and a T-shirt or a fancy dress, I'm still the same girl.

Wearing a school uniform would take away from my freedom of expression. I should be able to dress in ways that show who I am. Some days I'm in a blue mood; other days, I'm in a red mood. I'm never in a gray plaid mood. So why should I have to wear gray plaid skirts and white blouses every day? The idea is absurd! I would much rather wear cute, fun clothes than boring, ugly ones.

I've heard some people say that they want school uniforms because stylish clothes cost a lot of money. Okay, I understand that. My family isn't rich. I can't get everything I want. But I can get *some* things. I have a deal with my parents that if I want designer jeans, they'll buy me just one pair instead of two pairs of no-name jeans. I also know that I have to save my spending money in order to buy more expensive gym shoes. That's fair. My mom says it teaches me responsibility to have to make choices like that.

By the way, when do adults ever have to wear uniforms? Just in some jobs (where they get paid, by the way) like the military, food service, or hospitals.

My friends and I all agree that school uniforms are a really bad idea. Please don't take away our freedom to choose what we wear. Do us a favor: Forget all about uniforms at W.M.S.

Theresa Eldredge, 6th Grade

Washington Middle School

1. How can Theresa's attitude toward school uniforms be described best?

    A. a little negative
    B. strongly negative
    C. strongly positive
    D. neutral

2. Which statement best tells the main idea of the letter?

    A. I'm tired of hearing adults say that uniforms would make kids behave better.
    B. Mom says it teaches me responsibility to have to make choices like that.
    C. By the way, when do adults ever have to wear uniforms?
    D. My friends and I all agree that school uniforms are a really bad idea.

3. Read the following sentence from the passage.

    > I would much rather wear cute, fun clothes than boring, ugly ones.

    This statement is an example of which type of bad reasoning?

    A. a choice of two extremes
    B. circular reasoning
    C. unsupported inference
    D. oversimplifying

4. What assumption does Theresa make in the second paragraph?

    A. that school uniforms would be expensive
    B. that she only has red and blue moods
    C. that school uniforms would be in dull colors
    D. that kids wearing uniforms would behave well

5. Read this sentence from the passage.

    > The idea is <u>absurd</u>!

    What does the word *absurd* mean?

    A. funny
    B. healthy
    C. great
    D. crazy

6. Which of the following is a statement of fact?

    A. I should be able to dress in ways that show who I am.
    B. I have a deal with my parents.
    C. That's fair.
    D. School uniforms are a really bad idea.

7. Read this quote from the passage:

    My friends and I all agree that school uniforms are a really bad idea.

    Which propaganda technique is Theresa using in this quote?

    A. stereotyping
    B. snobbery
    C. bandwagon effect
    D. guilt by association

8. Is Theresa's reasoning in this letter well-supported? Why or why not? Use details from the passage to support your answer.

    _____

    _____

    _____

    _____

    _____

    _____

    _____

    _____

Lesson 11: Applying What You Read

Often in your reading you need to do more than simply understand the ideas in the passage. You also need to connect those ideas to your own knowledge and experiences, to other texts, and to circumstances in the "real world." You may also need to use the ideas in a passage to a new situation. This lesson will help you practice these important skills.

Personal Connections

When you read a passage, you don't just forget everything you know. You come to a passage with ideas and experiences of your own. The next two tips will help you practice seeing how personal background can affect your reading.

 TIP 1: Connect your life to the ideas in the passage.

As a sixth-grader, you have already collected a lot of life experiences. Those experiences will affect how you read. For example, the passage beginning on the following page is about superstitions. A **superstition** is a belief that has no facts behind it. If you have a few superstitions of your own—such as wearing a lucky hat or not stepping on cracks in the sidewalk—you might be interested to learn more about them. If your Aunt Pearl won't walk through a doorway unless she has done a little lucky dance first, you might think superstitions can be a bit silly. One question you might ask yourself is, *What experiences have I had that can help me to better understand this passage?*

1. Do you have any superstitions? If so, describe them.

   _____

   _____

   _____

2. Do you know others who have superstitions that are interesting or unusual? If so, describe them.

   _____

   _____

   _____

3. Why do you think people have superstitions?

_____

_____

_____

4. Does believing in superstitions "work"? Why or why not?

_____

_____

_____

⚠ Connecting a passage to your own experiences can be useful for understanding the writing and keeping your mind interested. Be careful, though, to keep straight which ideas are the author's and which are your own.

Read the following passage to learn about different kinds of superstitions. The passage will be used to help you understand the tips in this lesson.

Don't Step on That Crack!
by David McDonald

Don't walk under a ladder or misfortune will happen to you. Carry a silver dollar and you'll always be lucky. Don't take any unnecessary chances on Friday the 13th. Don't let a black cat cross your path. If you're having a winning streak in sports, don't change your socks. Do this, don't do that. The list of superstitions goes on and on.

Superstitions are traditions that have been passed down in every culture throughout the history of humankind. Each one connects an action with an event that is expected to happen in the future. They warn us of bad luck and tell us how to bring on good luck. They both frighten and calm us. And whether or not we believe in superstitions, most of us act as if we do—sometimes without even realizing it.

There are at least three general kinds of superstitions. Some may have a basis in fact, but most are simply based in fear.

Event superstitions have to do with the stages in a person's life. There are marriage superstitions (it's bad luck for a bride and groom to see each other before the wedding on the day of their marriage), birth superstitions (a baby born on Sunday will always be lucky), and death superstitions (after a person dies, the windows and doors of the room should be opened so that the spirit can leave). In fact, there are superstitions about nearly every important event that a person will experience in his or her lifetime.

Cause superstitions tell us that we can change our luck by taking certain actions. Some of these are so much a part of our culture that we don't even recognize them as superstitions anymore. Have you ever wondered why people throw rice at a wedding? This action isn't just a custom, it's a superstition. Supposedly, throwing rice at newlyweds ensures that they will have many children. Have you ever knocked on wood after saying that things are going well for you? Knocking on wood is supposed to ward off misfortune. Hanging a horseshoe like a U over a doorway is said to capture good luck—but don't let the horseshoe turn upside-down or your good luck will spill out.

Sign superstitions are supposed to foretell the future. Many people believe that breaking a mirror is a sign that you'll have seven years of bad luck. Finding a four-leaf clover, on the other hand, is a very lucky sign, indeed. Some sign superstitions can be canceled out (and turned into cause superstitions) if you quickly take a specific action. For example, spilling salt is considered to be a sign of bad luck ahead, but by immediately throwing a pinch of the salt over your shoulder, you might be able to escape your unhappy fate.

Once in a while, a superstition is found to be based at least partly in fact. Early in this century, some parents hung sacks of garlic around their children's necks to frighten away illness. Somehow, these children usually did stay healthy. The actual cause of their health may have had more to do with the smell of garlic than with any magical powers, however. Garlic has a strong odor that is offensive to some people. A child wearing garlic around the neck is less likely to come into contact with other people—sick *or* healthy. If you stay away from people and their germs, you are less likely to get sick. Did you know that there are tall buildings in the United States that don't have a 13th floor? Some people are so afraid of the number 13 that they won't visit an office or sleep in a hotel room on the 13th floor. Building managers try to make them feel better by numbering their floors 1 through 12, then 14 on up. The 13th floor is still there, it just has a different name! (In Japan, the unlucky number is four, not 13.)

The greatest danger connected with superstitions isn't what will happen if people don't pay attention to them, but what might happen if they *do*. Superstitions help some people cope with their fears by making them feel they are in control. But sometimes superstitions keep people from getting out and living a full life. That's when superstitious beliefs can do real harm. Superstitions can be fun and interesting, as long as you don't take them too seriously. After all, if having a rabbit's foot is supposed to bring good luck, keep in mind that it didn't work for the rabbit.

 TIP 2: Put yourself in another person's shoes.

Using what you have learned from the passage, try to imagine yourself in the situation the question presents. Look at the following example.

5. Which of these actions would be most like the things told about in this passage?

   A. a boy being punished after teasing his brother

   B. a girl climbing a tall ladder to get her cat off the roof

   C. a person crossing his or her fingers while making a wish

   D. a man taking care of a pet rabbit he found in the woods

Imagine yourself in each of the situations mentioned in the choices. In which situation would you most likely be trying to cause an event to happen?

Here are two more for you to try.

6. People who will not visit the 13th floor of a building are most likely to have which of the following characteristics?

   A. caution

   B. magical powers

   C. good health

   D. boldness

7. What experience most likely helped the author most in writing this passage?

   A. having rice thrown at him at a wedding

   B. letting a black cat cross his path

   C. being exposed to many kinds of common superstitions

   D. knocking on wood after saying he was having a good week

Applying Ideas

When you **apply** ideas, you transfer them from your reading to a new situation that is somehow similar. The information you are applying may help you to better understand something or to solve a problem. Ask yourself, *How can I use what I learned from my reading in this new situation?*

TIP 3: Read the question carefully.

When answering application questions, make sure to read the question carefully. The question will give you clues about where to search for the answer.

Read the following question, which has been printed without the answer choices. (Don't try to answer it yet.) Circle any key words in the question that may help you find the answer in the passage.

8. Which of the following is a cause superstition?

TIP 4: Skim the passage for key words from the question.

Once you have identified key words in the question, skim to find where they are located in the passage. Then read the information related to the key words.

9. Which paragraph will give you the most information about cause superstitions?

_____

_____

10. Based on the passage, what are the main characteristics of cause superstitions?

_____

_____

_____

TIP 5: Use information from the passage to make your choice.

Application questions ask you to apply ideas from the passage to a new situation. The correct answer, however, must be based on information from the passage. Any choices not supported by the passage should be dismissed before choosing your answer.

11. Look below at each of the answer choices for the question presented in Number 8.

     Which of the following is a cause superstition?

     A. If your nose itches, someone is thinking about you.

     B. A student takes all her tests with a certain "lucky" pen.

     C. When someone dies, all the mirrors in the house should be covered.

     D. Accidentally dropping a knife or fork means that company is coming.

You know the definition of a cause superstition from the passage. To choose the correct answer, go through all of the answer choices individually. Then decide which one best fits what you learned about cause superstitions.

 TIP 6: Connect your reading to related topics outside the passage.

Ask yourself how the passage relates to other topics. For example, superstitions are related to sports because athletes often use superstitions to build their confidence.

12. How might superstitions be related to medicine and maintaining health?

     _____

     _____

     _____

     _____

     _____

13. This passage contains information that could most help someone with which of the following?

     A. speaking Japanese

     B. playing a game of horseshoes

     C. attending a wedding

     D. avoiding getting a cold

TIP 7: Make predictions.

When you **predict**, you use what you already know to make a guess about something that might happen in the future.

14. How would this passage help someone who is traveling to Japan?

    A. It would help them know why there are no four-leaf clovers in Japan.

    B. It would help them know not to look for a 13th floor.

    C. It would help them understand any unusual things related to the number 4.

    D. It would help them understand why some children wear garlic to school.

15. Which of the following is the best example of someone letting superstitions keep him or her from "living a full life"?

    A. Lucinda throws salt over her shoulder after spilling some at dinner.

    B. Mike has looked all around but can't find a four-leaf clover.

    C. Megan can't find the 13th floor in a skyscraper in Atlanta.

    D. Tim postpones his wedding after seeing the bride on their wedding day.

16. How did the superstition about walking under a ladder most likely begin?

    A. Someone got hurt by standing on a ladder and falling.

    B. Someone saw a black cat walk under a ladder and broke her leg.

    C. Someone won a lot of money after walking under a ladder.

    D. Someone walked under a ladder and something bad happened.

17. "If your nose itches, you will kiss a fool" is what kind of superstition?

    A. a sign superstition

    B. a birth superstition

    C. an event superstition

    D. a marriage superstition

18. A baseball team is having a winning streak, and the pitcher says he has to wear his lucky cap in every game. This is an example of what kind of superstition?

    A. a sign superstition

    B. an event superstition

    C. a cause superstition

    D. a stage-of-life superstition

19. Which of the following is an example of an event superstition?

    A. Don't step on a crack or you will break your mother's back.

    B. If you make a wish on a falling star when you see it, your wish will come true.

    C. Find a penny, pick it up, and all day long you'll have good luck.

    D. A newborn must be carried upstairs before being carried downstairs.

Comparing Passages

You learned about comparing and contrasting parts of a single passage in Lesson 9. But sometimes you will need to connect ideas from two different passages. The following tips will help you practice this skill. First, read the next passage, and think about how it compares to "Don't Step on that Crack!"?

Read the following passage about two high school basketball stars and what they believe gives them an extra edge.

Hughes and Nantz lead Wolverines in semifinals tonight

by Minerva Plunkett, Staff Writer

LUMBERTON—In the girls' basketball state semifinals tonight, the City South Wolverines hope to defeat their opponents using speed and footwork. Coach Jane Hughes is known for getting her teams into top physical shape, and this year's team is no different.

Whether you're watching the game in the Capitol Arena, or from the comfort of your living room, you're sure to notice the team's co-captains, Samantha Hughes and Gabrielle Nantz. These two won top honors in the league and have been nominated for the all-state team.

But take away their socks and, according to the girls, "they stink." That is, the two swear that without their lucky anklets, they could not play well enough to start the game. "I don't even want to think about the possibility," says Nantz.

Like most superstitions, it didn't start out as one. Nantz says, "One day early in the season, we were changing for practice and discovered that we had the same brand of socks. That day, we just played really well. When the first game rolled around, we saw we were wearing the same socks again. It was like each of us had decided on our own, 'these are my lucky socks,' and saved them for the game."

If you're watching the girls tonight, you'll see the socks. You can't miss them. They are bright orange.

Jane Hughes is not bothered by her daughter's behavior, or by the violation of dress code. "People tell me it's just psychological. In this game, a psychological edge can mean the difference between winning and losing."

Jane Hughes herself wears a wristwatch taped to her skin for games. "The straps have been broken for—oh—seven years." She flashes a smile. "My mom was wearing this watch when my high school team won the state championship." Back then, she says, they were playing half-court ball.

Nantz's mother, Elaine, says she doesn't mind washing the socks for every game.

"You know how you always lose socks in the dryer?" she asks. "No way. Not these socks. Sometimes I've had to bring them to the game myself. But I would've come anyhow. The only problem I can see is they're getting holes in them. If it were up to me, I'd throw 'em away."

But that can't happen until the season is over, and the Wolverines hope that won't be tonight.

"Knowing Gabrielle, she'll want to save the socks if they win the tourney. Frame them and put 'em on the wall or something," Elaine Nantz says with a chuckle.

That would be a very small price to pay for the trophy the girls hope to gain.

But it's going a little too fast for Coach Hughes. "It's always one game at a time," she says. "That's one thing these superstitions do for the girls. They keep them focused on the here and now."

TIP 8: Make some general comparisons between the passages.

When comparing passages, notice how they are alike and different in a few basic ways, such as the following:

- **genre**, or type of passage
- topic, main idea, and theme
- **scope**, or range of information about the topic
- quality and amount of supporting details
- organization
- author's tone, attitude, and purpose

20. Can you think of other qualities to compare? If so, write them on the lines below.

_____

_____

_____

_____

_____

_____

Remember, when you **compare** two things, you are noticing how they are alike and different. When you **contrast** two things, you focus mainly on their differences.

Comparing Stories

When comparing two stories, look at how the following are alike or different:

- narrator, characters, and setting
- the main problem the characters face
- the main events
- how the problem is resolved
- the theme, or author's message
- the style in which the story is told

---

21. Complete the following graphic organizer to compare the two passages you have read in this lesson.

	Don't Step on That Crack!	Hughes and Nantz Lead Wolverines
What type of writing is it?		
What topic do the passages share?		
How much information does each passage give about the topic they share?	Circle one: A. a little B. a lot	Circle one: A. a little B. a lot
How is each passage organized?		
What is the author's tone and attitude toward superstitions?	A. positive B. negative C. neutral	A. positive B. negative C. neutral
What is the main idea of the passage?		

TIP 9: Think about how information from both passages can be connected.

Can information from one passage be applied to another? Can information from both passages be combined to help you gain a greater understanding? Questions such as these can help you make connections and gain more use from your reading.

22. Samantha and Gabrielle are following what type of superstition?

    A. event superstition

    B. cause superstition

    C. sign superstition

    D. health superstition

Following Directions

One common situation in which you must use application skills is when you follow directions. Instructions tell readers how to do things. They come in many forms—a recipe, a do-it-yourself book, a how-to article in a magazine, or step-by-step directions for putting something together. You might read instructions for many reasons:

- to follow directions
- to solve a problem
- to perform a procedure
- to answer questions

People who write instructions use certain text features to help you read and understand. Knowing about these features and following a few simple steps will help you better understand and follow instructions.

Read the following passage about making movies. It will help you with this lesson.

Making Movies
by Max Shadrach

Hollywood movies are expensive to make. A famous director such as Steven Spielberg can spend over $100 million making one of his features. But Spielberg started out making home movies as a boy in Arizona. Many of today's top filmmakers began by working in low-cost films for television, the foreign market, or what used to be the "drive-in" outdoor movies. Even you can make movies. Here's how.

Pre-Production

At the beginning of the filmmaking process, the most important creators are the producer, the director, and the writer. (Often on low-budget films, one person will do more than one job.) This early planning stage, called pre-production, may be the most important step. Poor planning can lead to major problems in filming. Pre-production involves writing the script, raising money, building sets or finding locations, and gathering a cast and crew.

The writer and director often work together on the script, or screenplay, which serves as a blueprint of the action and dialogue that will become the film. Each script must begin with characters (the people involved in the drama). A screenplay is divided into scenes (where and when the action takes place) and shots (the angles from which the action will be filmed). When the characters talk, that's dialogue. A take is what you record on film from the time you turn the camera on to the time you turn it off.

While the writer and director draft the screenplay, the producer must raise money for the budget (the total cost of making the movie). You don't need millions of dollars to make a home movie. When the crew and actors work for free, the costs of making a film are much lower. So how about a few hundred dollars? An enterprising young producer can often ask friends and family members for small amounts of money that add up to a nice budget.

The producer also works with the director to build sets and choose locations for shooting. It's important to have permission before showing up with a camera crew at a business or someone's home. The producer should get the approval of property owners before filming begins. If special sets are required, the producer oversees their construction. (On a small film, materials for building a set are probably where most of your budget will go.)

Last but not least, the director casts actors for the parts they will play in the film. If any more crew members are needed—such as a camera operator— the producer and director find people with the right skills for each job.

Production

Okay, you've got your script, you've raised the money, you've found your sets, and you've cast your actors. You're ready for production, for shooting the film. As they say in the movies: Lights! Camera! Action!

Filmmakers use a clapboard at the start of each take to identify it for the editor. There may be dozens of hours of raw footage, which are easier to organize if they are labeled. They use chalk to number each scene and take.

During production, the script is brought to life by the actors. The director helps the actors understand what to do in each scene and chooses the best way to film it. The cameraperson shoots the scenes, following the action with the camera. Each scene can be made up of many individual shots, and often each shot, or take, must be filmed many times to get it right. A filmmaker has to have patience!

There are several ways to save time and money. First, rehearse each scene with the actors before shooting any film. That way, the actors can practice their lines and blocking (how and where to move), and the director can guide the actors' performances. Rehearsal will lessen the number of wasted takes in which actors make mistakes.

Next, set up a shooting schedule. Because a film is put together in the editing room, directors can shoot scenes out of sequence. If certain sets or locations are available before others, shoot those scenes first. You may also need to set the schedule based on when actors or crewmembers can work.

As the movie is being made, the producer's role is to make sure things go smoothly, solving any problems that arise with locations, sets, the crew, and so on. On a small-scale movie, the producer may simply need to make sure there is enough film or videotape for each day's shooting.

Post-Production

Once your film is shot, you're ready to go into post-production. Often, this is when the filmmaker's money runs out. Remember to keep some of your budget for this important part of making the movie. There may be unexpected reshoots (filming a scene again to fix problems) or other hidden costs, such as adding special effects or renting an editing machine.

The editor receives all the footage (everything that has been shot, measured in feet of film or video tape). Working closely with the director, the editor then chooses the best take of each shot and assembles them into a whole movie. The editor has to pay close attention to rhythm and tempo—the flow and speed with which the story is told. A music soundtrack may be added, as well. (Do you have any friends who play music? They might provide your movie with an original score.) The movie is then put together into what is called a final cut, a version ready to be shown to an audience.

Many movies are first shown to test audiences to observe their reactions. People in the audience comment on what they like or don't like, and the director can use those comments to improve the film. Until it is sent out to a paying audience, a movie is considered a work-in-progress, so don't be afraid to make last-minute changes. After all, the goal of every filmmaker is to present the best film possible to the audience.

Making a movie takes a lot of work, but it can also be a lot of fun. With today's inexpensive digital video, which can be shot with a camera borrowed from a library and edited on a personal computer, young directors can make inexpensive movies at home while developing their skills. So, all you future Spielbergs, get started!

 TIP 10: Look at how the instructions are organized.

Before you begin reading the directions, look over the way the passage is organized. Longer instructions, like a computer manual or handbook, may have sections that give extra help. Is there a glossary to help you define terms? Is there a help section or index? Look at the table of contents and headings in the passage to see where the information is, and how it is organized.

23. How do the headings help organize the article?

    A. by defining important words in the text

    B. by dividing the text into the three stages of filmmaking

    C. by showing that pre-production is the most important step

    D. by giving readers filmmaking tips that the text itself does not

 TIP 11: Read through the passage carefully before you begin working.

Before you begin a project, read through the directions from beginning to end. Getting the "big picture" will help you know what to expect before you begin the process. You'll also get an idea about which steps are most important or may present the biggest challenge.

24. Skim back through "Making Movies." Why would someone read this article?

    A. to learn about different types of movies

    B. to follow directions for becoming a Hollywood star

    C. to learn about the big budgets that movies have

    D. to learn about how to make motion pictures

TIP 12: Gather all the materials listed.

Instructions often include a list of "Materials Needed." Sometimes, however, you may need to pull this information out of the passage on your own. As you read it for the first time, make a list of all the items you will need to complete the project, or review the list that is given to you. Then gather the items together in the area where you will be working. Having all your materials handy and ready to use will help make the project run smoothly.

25. Based on the passage, list the three items you would need to make a movie.

_____

 TIP 13: Follow the steps in order.

Most instructions list the steps of the project in the order in which they should be completed. When you begin working through the project, complete each step before going on to the next one. Also, be sure not to skip any steps. (You might check off each step as you complete it.) Following instructions carefully, completely, and in order will help you make the project a success.

26. What do you do after all the takes are filmed?

    A. Raise money.

    B. Write a screenplay.

    C. Make a shooting schedule.

    D. Put the scenes together.

 TIP 14: Pay close attention to the illustrations.

Always pay close attention to illustrations. Instructions often include diagrams and photographs that provide important information. They may contain information that the regular text does not. On the other hand, don't just look at the pictures and skip reading the text. Connect what you read in the text with what you see in the images to get a clear idea of the process.

27. What information does the illustration provide that the main text of "Making Movies" does not?

    A. A film editor begins with many takes of each shot.

    B. Shots and scenes in a movie are often filmed out of sequence.

    C. When raw footage has been edited, the result is the "final cut."

    D. Clapboards identify the director, cameraman, and date.

TIP 15: Take special note of highlighted words.

People who write instructions often use bold type, underlining, or capital letters to help you focus on important points. Notes, cautions, and warnings may be set off from the text in boxes. As you read the instructions, take special note of these highlighted parts.

 TIP 16: Be sure you understand specialized terms and symbols.

Instructions often include specialized terms and symbols. Often, manuals are written using specialized words. **Specialized words** are words that are only used for a specific topic. For example, a touchdown is a word only used when talking about football. While touchdown may be a popular specialized word, there are others that might be unfamiliar to you. Use the context clues you learned in Lesson 3 to help you understand specialized words. Look at the words around the unknown term for clues to its meaning. Also look for side bars, footnotes, illustrations, a glossary, and diagrams to help you define the word.

28. What is a scene?

    A. a board you use to organize a movie

    B. the money a movie earns from tickets

    C. where and when the action takes place

    D. a type of expensive movie camera

 TIP 17: Use information from the passage to make your choice.

Questions may ask you to apply ideas from the passage to a new situation. The correct answer must be based on information from the passage. Any choices not supported by the passage should be dismissed before choosing your answer.

Before answering the following question, cross out any choices that are not supported by the passage.

29. According to the passage, why are movies sometimes shown to test audiences?

    A. to get ideas from the audience for making the movie better

    B. to get ideas for making more movies like the one shown

    C. to ask the audience when the movie should be released

    D. to ask the audience to tell their friends about the movie

30. Which of these questions is answered by the passage?

   A. How can a moviemaker get the attention of Hollywood?

   B. Where are the best locations for shooting movie scenes?

   C. Why do directors sometimes shoot scenes out of order?

   D. How can someone learn acting and singing skills?

31. To save money in the production stage, the author recommends doing which of the following?

   A. film each shot many times until you get it right

   B. rehearse each scene and set up a shooting schedule

   C. do reshoots and have someone make an original score

   D. show the movie to test audiences and make changes

Reading Practice

Directions: Read the passage and answer the questions that follow.

How to Plant a Tree
by Karen Nichols

People often plant trees because they are beautiful to look at and pleasant to be around, but did you know that trees also play several important roles in our environment? For example, they absorb carbon dioxide and produce oxygen, helping to reduce global warming and pollution in the process. Trees lessen soil erosion and help improve the quality of our water supply. In addition, trees make life more comfortable by reducing temperatures with their shade, which lowers air conditioning costs for buildings nearby. Trees also help block and absorb the noise pollution that is common in cities. For all of these reasons, planting trees has become a popular service project for organizations, families, and individuals across the country.

With such important roles to play in our environment, new trees need the best start possible. By planting trees correctly, we can help them grow fast and live long. The following steps will walk you through the process.

Step 1: Choosing a place

A tree needs rich, well-drained soil and plenty of room to grow. Avoid planting very close to a building, where roots may harm pipes and foundations. Also, think about how tall your tree might grow, and see if any telephone or power wires will be in its way.

Whether you want to plant in a neighborhood park, on your school grounds, or in your own backyard, be sure to ask for permission from the property owner. Explain what kind of tree you want to plant and why. Some property owners may want only certain types of trees growing on their land.

Step 2: Choosing a tree

The tree you choose must be well suited to the environment in which it is planted. Will it thrive in the climate of your area? Palm trees don't last very long in Alaska, and orange trees won't make it in Maine.

Your choice will also depend on your purpose for the tree. Do you want a tree that gives plenty of shade? Then choose one with a lot of leaves, such as a maple, oak, or ash. Do you want a tree that will beautify a garden, yard, or park? If so, you might look for a flowering tree, such as a crab apple, dogwood, or magnolia. Do you want a row of trees that will block cold winter winds from your home? Then consider needleleafs or cottonwoods. Do you want a tree that produces fruit? Then maybe an apple, cherry, pear, peach, fig, or citrus tree would be right for you.

You can plant with seeds, which take a long time to grow. Most people, however, choose to buy a young tree from a nursery. Some organizations donate trees for tree-planting projects; contact your local forester for resources in your area.

Step 3: Planting the tree

It is best to plant in the fall, winter, or early spring, when the tree is "resting." Once it is planted, the tree will be ready to "wake up" and focus on growing in the warmer spring and summer months, when it can gather plenty of energy from the sun.

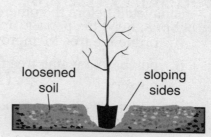

Figure 1

Dig a hole as deep as the roots and twice as wide. (See Figure 1.) The hole should allow plenty of room for all the roots. Loosen up the surrounding soil with a shovel so that the roots can break through the soil more easily.

Remove the tree from the container and gently loosen up the roots a bit. (Handle the tree by the roots, not by the trunk or branches.) Place the tree in the hole so that the soil is at the same level on the tree as it was in the container. If the roots are covered with burlap, carefully untie the burlap after placing the tree in the hole. (It is okay to leave the burlap in the hole; it will break down and become part of the soil over time.)

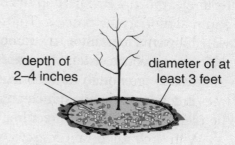

Figure 2

Fill in the hole around the tree with soil. No roots should be sticking up above ground level. Pack the soil firmly. Use any leftover soil to create a "wall" about two or three inches high circling the tree at the edge of the hole. This will help direct water to the roots. Water the tree—really give it a good soaking. You may wish to support your tree with stakes to keep it from blowing over in a strong wind.

Place a covering of wood chips, pine straw, or bark chips around—but not touching—the base of the tree. Make the layer two to four inches deep and at least three feet wide. (See Figure 2.) This layer, called mulch, will help keep too much water from evaporating out of the soil. Mulch also helps keep weeds away and helps protect the tree roots from the cold.

Step 4: Caring for the tree

Give your tree a deep watering every week until it is well rooted, about a year from when it was planted. (You can skip weeks when the tree gets a good amount of rainfall.)

You may wish to prune, or trim, your tree to improve its shape. Cutting off some of the lower buds will keep it from growing low branches. Leave enough buds, however, to allow the tree to grow full.

Watch for signs of insects or disease. Most likely, your tree will be able to withstand these attacks. If the tree begins to look unhealthy—developing fewer or unusually pale leaves—consider seeking professional help. Call your local nursery, describe the trouble, and ask for advice.

If you carefully follow these steps, your tree should grow strong and healthy, providing beauty and shade for years to come.

1. Which of the following steps should be completed before the others?

   A. prune the tree to improve its shape

   B. purchase a young tree from a nursery

   C. ask permission from the property owner

   D. dig a hole that is as deep as the roots

2. Jill wants to plant a tree in honor of her newborn sister. She wants the tree to be big enough for her sister to climb in ten years or so. Which step should Jill take to help her meet her goal?

   A. purchase a young tree from her local nursery

   B. get tree seeds from a free-tree program

   C. purchase maple tree seeds from her local forester

   D. purchase magnolia tree seeds from her local nursery

3. When planting a tree, you will most likely need all of the following items except which one?

   A. shovel

   B. mulch

   C. water

   D. burlap

4. What information do the illustrations provide that the directions do not?

   A. how big to make the hole

   B. how the sides of the hole should slope

   C. how wide and deep to place the mulch

   D. how the soil surrounding the hole should be loosened

5. Read these sentences from the passage.

   Watch for signs of insects or disease. Most likely, your tree will be able to withstand these attacks.

   What does the word *withstand* mean?

   A. weaken

   B. survive

   C. return

   D. notice

6. Which of the following would be the best way to preview this passage?

    A. Skim the first sentence of each paragraph.

    B. Read the last paragraph, then summarize it in your mind.

    C. Skim the passage for words that you don't know, then look them up in a dictionary.

    D. Read the title, subheadings, illustrations, sidebar, and boldfaced words.

7. Describe two ways trees improve the environment. Use details from the passage to support your answer.

_____

_____

_____

_____

_____

_____

_____

_____

_____

Lesson 12: Finding Out More

Do you remember the last time you wanted to learn more about a topic that interested you? Where did you look for information—an encyclopedia? An atlas? An almanac? A person who is an expert on the topic? Somewhere else?

You can use many different resources to find information. A **resource** is something that gives you information: usually a book or passage. As you go through school, you'll get to know them well. In fact, you'll use resources to find information throughout your life.

This lesson will give tips to help you not only in the research you do for school, but also in answering the kinds of resource questions you're likely to see on a reading test.

 TIP 1: Use what you know about library reference materials.

The **reference section** of your school library is one of the best places to start looking for information about any topic. There you'll find encyclopedias, dictionaries, almanacs, and many other helpful materials. Here are some of the kinds of resources that are most useful in finding out just about anything you need to know.

Almanacs

An **almanac** is published every year and contains up-to-date facts about all kinds of topics. Much of the information in an almanac is printed in the form of lists. The information is updated once every year.

Use an almanac to find facts from a particular year, such as . . .

- names of people inducted into the Baseball Hall of Fame

- major export products of the United States

- important events that took place during a certain year

- number of votes each presidential candidate received in the last election

- real names of actors and movie stars

- names of movies that won Academy Awards

Atlases

An **atlas** is a book of maps. Some atlases show maps of one part of the world, such as the *Rand McNally Road Atlas: United States, Canada, and Mexico*. Others include maps of the entire world. In addition, many atlases have a specific focus. For example, a road atlas shows all the roads in an area, and a historical atlas shows where important historical events took place.

Use an atlas to find the location of . . .

- borders and boundaries (between counties, states, nations, etc.)

- bodies of water (oceans, glaciers, rivers, lakes, etc.)

- land formations (continents, mountain ranges, deserts, plains, etc.)

- population facts (cities, countries, etc.)

1. What do you think the *World Ocean Atlas* shows?

_____

Other than new volcanoes or huge earthquakes, few major changes occur in the world's landscape from year to year. But important political changes take place from time to time. Nations gain or lose territory in wars. Leaders rename cities—or even entire nations. To keep up with the most recent changes, you'll need a current atlas.

Dictionaries

A **dictionary** is a book filled with definitions of the words that make up a language. It doesn't change much from year to year, although a few new words are added from time to time. An American English dictionary contains the English words that are spoken in the United States. A Spanish/English dictionary gives Spanish words and their equivalents in English.

Use a dictionary to find:

- correct spellings

- definitions

- parts of speech (such as whether a word is used as a verb, a noun, or an adjective)

- word origins (what other language or languages the word came from)

Here is an example of a dictionary entry:

> **kudos**   (kōō' dōz'), *n*. [Gk. *kydos*, praise] (1831) 1. fame resulting from an act or achievement; prestige 2. praise given for an act or achievement: *The actor received many kudos for her performance.*

In addition to giving the definition and pronunciation of *kudos*, we are told that the word is a noun, that it comes from a Greek word meaning "praise," and that it first appeared in print in English in 1831. The entry also gives an example of the word as it is used in a sentence.

Glossaries

A **glossary** gives a list of specialized terms and their meanings. Glossaries are often found in textbooks. A glossary entry looks similar to a dictionary entry. The following is a glossary entry from a mathematics textbook.

> **equation**   Any number sentence that contains an equal sign (=)

Thesauruses

A **thesaurus** is a book of words and their synonyms. If you want to find a word that means about the same thing as *reckless*, reach for a thesaurus.

> **reckless**, *adj*. careless, foolhardy, incautious, heedless, rash. *See rashness, neglect.*

Answer the following questions by writing "D" for dictionary, "G" for glossary, or "T" for thesaurus in the blank after each question.

_____   2.   Imagine you are reading a science textbook when you come across the word *microbe*. Where would be the most convenient place to find a definition of *microbe*?

_____   3.   Where would be the best place to look for a word that has the same meaning as *cooperation*?

_____   4.   What resource would help you find out how to pronounce *virtuoso*?

Encyclopedias

An **encyclopedia** contains facts and explanations about a wide variety of subjects. It also has drawings, diagrams, maps, and photographs. Topics are arranged in alphabetical order.

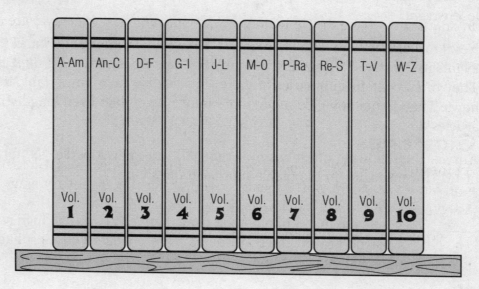

Some encyclopedias, such as *The World Book Encyclopedia* or *The New Encyclopaedia Britannica*, contain information about almost every subject you could think of. Others, such as *The Encyclopedia of Dogs* or *The Encyclopedia of Medicine*, are more narrowly focused on very specific topics.

An encyclopedia can provide more information than a dictionary or atlas, but it may not contain the most current information on a topic.

Newspapers

Most **newspapers** are printed once a day. Newspapers contain very current news updates. Newspaper articles may be brief or in-depth, depending on their importance to the community and the amount of information available about the topic. Newspapers also frequently contain "feature stories" telling about things of interest to the community, including events, people, businesses, hobbies, products, and so on.

Magazines

Magazines usually focus on a particular topic, such as news, famous people, hobbies, or sports. If you read an article from *Cooking Light*, for example, you would expect to find recipes designed for people who are health-conscious or who want to lose weight.

News magazines such as *Newsweek* and *Time* contain information about important events in the news. Magazines are published less frequently than most newspapers. They often contain summaries of the events leading up to important stories in the news. They frequently give much more information than even lengthy newspaper articles do.

Answer the following questions by writing "E" for encyclopedia, "N" for newspaper, or "M" for magazine in the blank after each question.

_____ 5. Imagine that a big football game between two rival high schools was played in your town last night. Where would you most likely be able to read about the game?

_____ 6. Imagine that an exchange student is coming to your school from South Africa, and your teacher wants you to learn about the student's country. What resource would give you a good general overview of South Africa?

_____ 7. If you wanted to learn tips about cross-country bicycle touring and read articles by people who have gone biking in different places, what would be the best resource to use?

Computers

You can use **computers** to find information in a variety of sources:

- **CD-ROMs** are compact discs containing information that can be read by a computer. Encyclopedias and dictionaries are just two types of resources that can be found on CD-ROM.

- An **electronic database** is a collection of information organized in such a way that you can easily find the data you need. Many schools use databases to store information about students, such as their full names, ages, parents' names, addresses, and phone numbers.

- The **Internet** is a network of computers around the world. Information about almost any topic can be found on the Internet. One way to search for information on the Net is by using a **search engine**, such as Google or Yahoo, to search for key words. The search engine pulls up a list of addresses for **websites** that contain the words you searched for. Other resources, such as encyclopedias, dictionaries, thesauruses, and news services, also can be found on the Internet.

8. If you were doing research about space travel, NASA's website would be most useful for finding

   A. detailed information on recent missions.

   B. an article on astronauts from Mississippi.

   C. a timeline of Russian cosmonauts.

   D. a story about a boy who dreams of spaceflight.

Library Catalogs

A library catalog tells where to find the materials in the library—books, videotapes, music CDs, and so on—so that people can easily find them. The catalog may come in either of two forms: a computer database or a collection of paper cards with printed information. It includes important information about the materials, such as the author, date of publication, publisher, and content.

Every book has a unique **call number**—a label made up of a series of numbers and letters. Or, the label may just tell the section of the library (such as juvenile fiction) and the author's last name. Once you know the call number of the item you need, just follow the signs (usually posted on the shelves) to find the item's location in the library.

Card Catalog   Computer Catalog

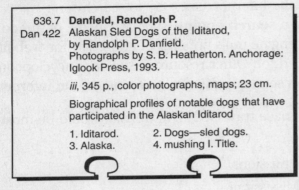

```
636.7      Danfield, Randolph P.
Dan 422    Alaskan Sled Dogs of the Iditarod,
           by Randolph P. Danfield.
           Photographs by S. B. Heatherton. Anchorage:
           Iglook Press, 1993.

           iii, 345 p., color photographs, maps; 23 cm.

           Biographical profiles of notable dogs that have
           participated in the Alaskan Iditarod

           1. Iditarod.        2. Dogs—sled dogs.
           3. Alaska.          4. mushing I. Title.
```

```
636.7
Dan 422
─────────────────────────────────────────
     AUTHOR   Danfield, Randolph P.
      TITLE   Alaskan Sled Dogs of the
              Iditarod; photographs by S.B.
              Heatherton.
  PUBLISHER   Anchorage: Iglook Press, 1993.
DESCRIPTION   iii, 345 p., color photographs,
              maps; 23 cm.
       NOTE   Biographical profiles of notable
              dogs that have participated in the
              Alaskan Iditarod.
    SUBJECT   Iditarod. Dogs—sled dogs.
              Alaska. mushing.
   LOCATION   Adult non-fiction
     STATUS   Checked in
CALL NUMBER   636.7/Dan 422
```

Card catalogs are arranged alphabetically by author, title, and subject matter. Each book in the library will have at least those three cards. The card shown is listed by the author, Randolph Danfield. It could also be located by looking up the title, *Alaskan Sled Dogs of the Iditarod*, or the subject matter: sled dogs, or Alaska.

9. What other information is given on the catalog card?

    _____

    _____

10. What information does the computer catalog provide that the catalog card cannot?

    _____

TIP 2: Consider what other sources of information might be helpful in researching a topic.

There are many good ways to learn about a topic. Keep an open mind when you are researching, and brainstorm as many possible sources of information as you can.

11. Review the list of resources below. Can you think of other possible resources in addition to those listed? Brainstorm with your classmates to come up with ideas.

_____

_____

A **biography** is a book about someone's life. An **autobiography** is a book a person writes about his or her own life.

A **brochure** (also known as a **pamphlet**) is a very short booklet that tells about one main topic, such as treating the symptoms of the common cold or what you can see at Great Smoky Mountains National Park.

A **directory** is a list of information, usually on a single topic. A telephone directory lists all the telephone numbers within a certain calling area. A directory of United States military bases would tell the names, locations, and a few facts about all of the bases run by the U.S. military.

A **manual** is a set of instructions telling how to use and care for a product, such as a computer game or a walkie-talkie set.

Textbooks are designed to be used by students and teachers who are studying a specific subject. Textbooks have been written on almost every topic you can imagine, and many can be found on library shelves.

People can be excellent resources. If you want to find out what you have to do to become a NASCAR driver, you can talk to someone who has driven in one of the races. He or she will probably be able to give tips that you'd never find printed in any racing handbook.

An **essay** is a discussion of a topic much shorter than a book.

An **editorial** is an essay published in the opinion section of a newspaper that gives the writer's viewpoint on an issue.

An **infomercial** is a television program that is really a long advertisement for a product or service.

A **journal** or **diary** records a person's thoughts and experiences, often for personal use only.

A **newsletter** is a small publication that contains information of interest to a specific group of people. Some schools send out monthly newsletters informing parents about policies, news, and events at the school.

Authors often include helpful resources with their writing, such as illustrations, diagrams, maps, photos, tables, charts, sidebars, and so on. Pay close attention to these resources, and think about how they might add to your understanding of the passage.

 TIP 3: Decide whether you want to use a primary or secondary source.

Most resources fall into one of the following categories:

- **Primary sources** are direct sources. A primary source is created by someone who has "been there" or "done that." A letter written by a soldier to his wife during the Civil War is an example of a primary source.

- **Secondary sources** are indirect sources. A secondary source is created by someone who wasn't "there," but has researched the people who were. A history book describing the important battles of the Civil War is an example of a secondary source.

Use primary resources for first-hand information about your topic. If you're writing about how the Civil War affected marriages, the soldier's letter to his wife would be a very helpful resource.

Use secondary resources when you need a more unbiased (open-minded) look at your topic. Someone who has "been there" is going to bring some biases to the topic, but someone who wasn't there may show all sides of the topic.

Sometimes, you will want to use a combination of primary and secondary resources. You can also use secondary resources to better understand what was going on when an author created a primary resource.

Practice Activity 1

Directions: Following is a list of sources that a student is planning to use for a report about the history of Mexico. Label each source with "P" for "Primary" or "S" for "Secondary."

_____   1. an encyclopedia entry for the word *Mexico*

_____   2. a chapter in a history textbook about early Mexican civilizations such as the Aztecs

_____   3. a letter written by a Mexican woman to her husband, a soldier fighting against the United States in the Mexican War

_____   4. photos of important historical sites in Mexico

_____   5. an Internet website that gives a brief history of Mexico during the 20th century

_____   6. a copy of a speech by the current Mexican president

 TIP 4: Use text features to locate important information in a resource.

Many authors will include **text features** to help the reader better understand the writing. Text features include unit and chapter titles, headings, and subheadings or phrases that organize the information within the text and tell the reader what to expect. Other features, such as the table of contents, preface, appendix, index, and bibliography can be useful in locating specific ideas in a larger book.

The best place to start is the table of contents. A **table of contents** shows how the book (or magazine or newspaper) is organized by listing the first page of the introduction, each chapter, and any other sections of the book.

Read the following table of contents from a book called *The Gold Medal Guide to Olympic Sports*.

Table of Contents

12. In which chapter would you most likely find information about figure skaters?

A. 1

B. 4

C. 6

D. 8

The **preface** is an introduction to a work often written by the author to explain what the work is about. The author may use the preface to explain to the reader why he or she chose a given topic.

Many books contain an **appendix**, a section of material that supports the main body of the text. An appendix may contain tables or graphs, additional articles, or other information. Appendices are generally found in the backs of books.

An **index** is an alphabetical list of all the important topics in a book, along with the page numbers where each topic can be found. If you want to find a piece of information about speed skater Apollo Anton Ono in *The Gold Medal Guide to Olympic Sports*, find his name in the index.

A **bibliography** is a list of all of the sources that an author consulted or quoted as he or she was writing his or her own work. Each entry in the bibliography usually includes the title, author, publisher, publication date, and page number where the author found the information that he or she used.

Use the excerpt from an index page of *The Gold Medal Guide to Olympic Sports* to answer Number 13.

13. On what page of *The Gold Medal Guide to Olympic Sports* would you find information about alpine skier Francisco Ochoa?

A. 14

B. 154

C. 212

D. 374

oath	14
O'Brien, Dan	271, 326
Ochoa, Francisco	154
Oda, Mikio	212
Olympic village	21, 56, 133
Ono, Apollo Anton	374, 376
Oslo, Norway	85, 126–128
Ottenbrite, Anne	77, 113
Otto, Kristin	321, 350
Owens, Jesse	60–62, 112

Captions are brief descriptions that accompany illustrations. A caption may identify the subject of a photograph, explain an illustration, or give some additional information about what is pictured. (See the photo for an example.)

A cluster of galaxies called Abell 2218, as photographed by the Hubble Space Telescope

You can also use topic sentences and concluding sentences to find information quickly. In informational articles, such as those found in encyclopedias, the first and last sentences of each paragraph often state what the paragraph is about. If you are looking for a specific fact about a subject, reading the topic and concluding sentences of each paragraph will help you locate a detail without having to read the entire article.

TIP 5: Summarize and combine information from more than one source.

When you are using sources to research a topic, summarize what you read. Break down the information from each source into the most important points and details. Put together all these facts and opinions on your topic, everything you know about it. You can use these chunks of knowledge to support your own writing on the subject.

Answering Resource Questions

In addition to using resources to find out more about a topic, you will sometimes need to answer questions about resources on a state test. The following four tips can help answer these kinds of questions.

TIP 6: Read resource questions carefully.

Of course, the first step is to read the question carefully to be sure of what it is asking. Some common types of resource questions might include the following:

What would be the best way to find out more about the topic of the passage?

What would be the best way to make sure the information in this passage is correct?

Which resource would most help a reader to understand this passage?

TIP 7: Determine the main topic that you're being asked about.

Next, your job is to figure out the passage's main topic and its "angle," or the way it approaches the topic. Finding the topic is only part of the job here—you also need to decide how the author has treated the topic.

Imagine that you've just finished reading a passage about legendary basketball star Michael Jordan's brief try at professional baseball in the 1990s. It tells about Jordan's positive attitude and the public's warm response as he unsuccessfully attempted to fulfill one of his childhood dreams. (Michael quit baseball to complete his outstanding career as a professional basketball player for the Chicago Bulls and later the Washington Wizards, finally retiring for good in 2003.)

After reading the passage, you come to the following question (look at it, but don't answer it yet).

14. Which of these articles would most help a reader to understand the passage?

    A. "The Early Days of Baseball History"

    B. "Jordan Scores Big in Basketball"

    C. "Baseball's Greatest Record Breakers"

    D. "Baseball Loses but Jordan Wins Our Hearts"

The passage is all about something that happened in the history of baseball. But that alone won't help you find the correct answer choice, since most of the choices deal with baseball. The topic's angle is to describe a popular basketball player who tried, unsuccessfully, to switch to baseball.

 TIP 8: Decide what type of resource each answer choice represents.

The answer choices will often give clues about what type of reference materials they are and what they contain. If you see a title that suggests the source is a newspaper, you'll know that the information will be timely and factual. Likewise, if you see a title that sounds like a biography, you can expect information about one person's life story.

Remember, too, that the titles of books, movies, and magazines are printed in italics, while the titles of articles, brochures (pamphlets), and stories are printed in regular type within quotation marks.

Look again at Number 14. All of the answer choices are articles, so they are all in quotation marks. If *Yer Out! Baseball's Weirdest and Wackiest Stories* was one of the choices, you would know that it has to be a book, movie, or magazine title. Based on the title, you can guess that it is probably a book. If "Michael's Baseball Adventure" were one of the choices, you would know that it has to be an article, brochure, or story. Based on the title, you can guess that it is a story.

Practice Activity 2

Directions: Look at the following list. On the line after each title or name, tell what kind of resource it is. (Look back at the list of resources in this lesson if you need help.)

1. *Compton's Pictured Encyclopedia* _____

2. *Webster's New World Dictionary* _____

3. *TV Guide* _____

4. *The Man Who Invented Baseball: The Life of Abner Doubleday* _____

5. *Children's Museums of the Northern Hemisphere* _____

6. "Your Guide to the Public Library" _____

7. *National Geographic World* _____

8. *United States Road Atlas* _____

9. scientist James Van Allen _____

TIP 9: Look for the answer choice that would give the best information about the topic.

Once you have carefully read the question, figured out the topic, and decided what type of resource each choice represents, you are ready to choose. The answer choice that seems to be most closely related to the passage's "angle" is probably the right choice.

Let's look at Number 14 one last time. Keep in mind that the passage's angle is to describe a popular basketball player who tried, unsuccessfully, to switch to baseball.

14. Which of these articles would most help a reader to understand the passage?

    A. "The Early Days of Baseball History"
    B. "Jordan Scores Big in Basketball"
    C. "Baseball's Greatest Record Breakers"
    D. "Baseball Loses but Jordan Wins Our Hearts"

You know that the passage is about someone who played baseball in the 1990s, which rules out A. You also know that the passage is not about his basketball career, but rather his short-lived baseball career, ruling out B. You also know that Jordan was not very successful when he played baseball, which rules out C. Finally, you know that everyone enjoyed Jordan's spirited attempt at baseball, and welcomed him back to basketball. The correct choice has to be D.

Let's try it again, with a fresh question this time. The following question is based on a passage about hunting for wild mushrooms to cook for dinner. Read the question and look for the best answer choice.

15. What would be the best way to find out if the information in the passage is correct?

    A. Read *Surviving in the Wilderness: How to Know What's Safe to Eat.*
    B. Look at famous paintings that picture mushrooms.
    C. Read *The Wonderful Flight to the Mushroom Planet* by Eleanor Cameron.
    D. Look up the word *mushroom* in a dictionary.

All of the choices would probably tell you something about mushrooms. But which choice would tell the *most* about hunting for wild mushrooms that you could cook for dinner? Choice B may be nice to look at, but won't offer any facts about mushrooms. Choice C could be a fun story about mushrooms, but it won't give you any "real world" information about them. Choice D may give you some good general information about mushrooms, but only A can tell you which kinds are safe to eat.

Reading Practice

Directions: Read the passage and answer the questions that follow.

New Uses for an Old Tradition
by Jane Minturn

Aikido is a martial art, which means it is a system of self-defense. Aikido, however, is different from most martial arts. It does not teach any hitting, punching, or bone-breaking techniques.[1] Aikido may be the best, or truest, form of self-defense. People who practice aikido never attack. They only defend themselves against their opponent's moves.

Ueshiba Morihei

The goal of aikido is to remove the idea of fighting from the attacker's mind. Aikido teaches people how to do this by showing them how to move out of the line of attack. It also shows people how to overcome attackers by turning their own punches and kicks against them. In this way, an attacker hurts only himself. He soon gives up the idea of fighting.

Although aikido probably originated in Japan during the 14th century, it was developed in the early 20th century by Ueshiba Morihei. Ueshiba was a devoted student of the martial arts throughout his life. He eventually learned several martial art forms, including jujitsu, judo, sword fighting, and stick fighting. In jujitsu, he learned to use his body as a weapon of warfare, a tool for killing or seriously hurting an opponent. In judo, he learned techniques of using his body to apply pressure to an opponent's neck or arm joints to gain an advantage. In stick fighting and sword fighting, Ueshiba learned to use weapons to fight to the death. Each of these forms of martial arts was intended to be used in warfare.

Ueshiba felt something was missing from his training. He thought martial arts should be a way of life and not just a means of combat. He developed aikido by putting together what he knew about the other martial arts with his ideas about inner peace and calmness. Ueshiba believed that love and harmony are the basic principles of life. Training the mind to achieve inner calmness is an important part of aikido. Before a person can master aikido, he or she must learn how to make the mind and body work together. Masters of judo, jujitsu, and other martial arts also emphasize the mind-body connection. The difference, however, is that Ueshiba's aikido also teaches the value of peacefulness and harmony.

Ueshiba is no longer alive, but his many students continue to pass on the art of aikido. Ueshiba himself claimed to never be more than a student of aikido. He was a very modest man who always tried to improve himself and help others.

[1] **technique:** the way a task is completed or accomplished

1. What is the author's purpose for writing this passage?

    A. to encourage people to learn self defense

    B. to inform the reader about aikido and its founder

    C. to prove that aikido is the best form of martial arts

    D. to entertain with a story about a man's life and work

2. What source would be best to provide general information about aikido?

    A. an almanac

    B. a thesaurus

    C. a dictionary

    D. an encyclopedia

3. Which detail best supports the idea that aikido is based on defense?

    A. Ueshiba Morihei founded aikido.

    B. Aikido is a very old tradition.

    C. People who use aikido never attack.

    D. Aikido probably originated in the 14th century.

4. If you wanted to find out about other types of martial arts, where would be the best place to look?

    A. a thesaurus

    B. an atlas

    C. a reference book

    D. a health magazine

5. Read this sentence from the passage.

    Although aikido probably <u>originated</u> in Japan during the 14th century, it was developed in the early 20th century by Ueshiba Morihei.

    The word *originated* means

    A. began.

    B. taught.

    C. worked.

    D. stopped.

6. What is the purpose of footnotes in this passage?

    A. to give the meaning of difficult words

    B. to show which sources the author used

    C. to show which words come from other languages

    D. to give the correct pronunciation of a word

7. In the word *calmness* in paragraph 4, what does the suffix "ness" mean?

    A. the study of

    B. happening every so often

    C. lacking something

    D. the state of being something

8. How is aikido different than other martial arts? Use details from the passage to support your answer.

_____

_____

_____

_____

_____

_____

_____

_____

Notes

Notes

Notes

Notes